REVELS PLAYS

THE JEW OF MALTA
Christopher Marlowe

MANCHESTER
1824

Manchester University Press

REVELS STUDENT EDITIONS

Based on the highly respected Revels Plays, which provide a wide range
of scholarly critical editions of plays by Shakespeare's contemporaries,
the Revels Student Editions offer readable and competitively priced
introductions, text and commentary designed to distil the erudition and
insights of the Revels Plays, while focusing on matters of clarity and
interpretation. These editions are aimed at undergraduates, graduate
teachers of Renaissance drama and all those who enjoy the vitality and
humour of one of the world's greatest periods of drama.

GENERAL EDITOR David Bevington

Dekker/Rowley/Ford *The Witch of Edmonton*
Fletcher *The Tamer Tamed; or, The Woman's Prize*
Ford *'Tis Pity She's a Whore*
Jonson *Bartholomew Fair*
Jonson *Volpone*
Jonson *Masques of Difference: Four Court Masques*
Kyd *The Spanish Tragedy*
Marlowe *The Jew of Malta*
Marlowe *Tamburlaine the Great*
Marston *The Malcontent*
Middleton *Women Beware Women*
Middleton/Rowley *The Changeling*
Middleton/Tourneur *The Revenger's Tragedy*
Webster *The Duchess of Malfi*
Webster *The White Devil*

Plays on Women: An Anthology
Middleton *A Chaste Maid in Cheapside*
Middleton/Dekker *The Roaring Girl*
Anon. *Arden of Faversham*
Heywood *A Woman Killed with Kindness*

REVELS STUDENT EDITIONS

THE JEW OF MALTA
Christopher Marlowe

Edited by David Bevington

based on The Revels Plays edition
edited by N. W Bawcutt
published by Manchester University Press, 1978

MANCHESTER
UNIVERSITY PRESS
Manchester and New York

distributed in the United States exclusively by
Palgrave Macmillan

Introduction, critical apparatus, etc.
© David Bevington 1997

The right of David Bevington to be identified as the editor of this work
has been asserted by him in accordance with the Copyright, Designs and
Patents Act 1988.

Published by Manchester University Press
Oxford Road, Manchester M13 9NR, UK
and Room 400, 175 Fifth Avenue, New York, NY 10010, USA
www.manchesteruniversitypress.co.uk

Distributed in the United States exclusively by
Palgrave Macmillan, 175 Fifth Avenue, New York,
NY 10010, USA

Distributed in Canada exclusively by
UBC Press, University of British Columbia, 2029 West Mall,
Vancouver, BC, Canada V6T 1Z2

British Library Cataloguing-in-Publication Data
A catalogue record for this book is available from the British Library

Library of Congress Cataloging-in-Publication Data applied for

ISBN 978 0 7190 5180 7 *paperback*

First published 1997

16 15 14 13 12 11 10 09 08   10 9 8 7 6 5 4

Printed in Great Britain
by Bell & Bain Ltd, Glasgow

Introduction

Machiavel, in his gloating Prologue to this play, remarks that 'the Guise' is now dead (l. 3). The phrasing suggests an event of recent date. The infamous Duke of Guise, who had ordered the slaughter of French Huguenots in 1572, was assassinated on 23 December 1588. Probably, then, Marlowe wrote this play in 1589 or 1590. It was first performed in early 1592 at the Rose theatre, and was a success. A revival in 1594 may have capitalized on the hysteria surrounding the trial and execution of Queen Elizabeth's Jewish physician, Dr Lopez, on charges of conspiring the Queen's death. Marlowe's own sensational death in 1593, combined with his reputation as a blasphemer and nonconformist, may well have added to the play's notoriety. It remained popular well into the next century, until the closing of the theatres in 1642, and was acted at court in or before 1633.

Stephen Gosson mentions a play called *The Jew* that was shown at the Bull in 1579 or earlier, 'representing the greediness of worldly choosers and bloody minds of usurers' (*The School of Abuse*, fol. C6v). A later play by William Rowley, *A Search for Money* (1609), portrays a repulsive usurer with 'an old moth-eaten cap buttoned under his chin, his visage (or vizard) like the artificial Jew of Malta's nose' (Percy Society edition, 1840, p. 19), suggesting that the actor playing Barabas wore a large false nose; see II.iii.176, III.iii.9–10, and IV.i.25 for references to Barabas's nose in Marlowe's text. Whether the practice was general on the Elizabethan stage has been challenged recently by James Shapiro (*Shakespeare and the Jews*, 1995), and we cannot tell from Shakespeare's *The Merchant of Venice* (*c.* 1596–7) if Shylock was caricatured as Jewish in appearance other than by his gaberdine, but Marlowe's play at least does seem to invite hostile if also admiring laughter at the expense of the protagonist.

Barabas is not the first Jew to appear in an English play. A late fifteenth-century religious play, the Croxton *Play of the Sacrament*, features five Jews who subject the sacred host of the Mass to torture reminiscent of Christ's crucifixion, only to be converted to Christianity when they discover that Christ is truly present in that sacrament. The Jews in the religious cycle plays are generally represented as the persecutors of Christ. Although the animus against Jews in English Renaissance drama after the Reformation is not as strident, the prejudice persists. Gerontus the Jew in *The Three Ladies of London* (*c.* 1581) is a usurer in a play that inveighs against usury, albeit less grasping than some Christian moneylenders. *The Jew of Malta* reminds its audience of virulently anti-Semitic stories of the supposed kidnapping and crucifying of children by Jews, of poisoning wells, and the like. 'What, has he crucified a child?' asks Friar Jacomo in reference to Barabas, only to be answered, 'No, but a worse thing' (III.vi.49–50). 'Sometimes I go about and poison wells', Barabas boasts to Ithamore (II.iii.179).

A common theme in the representation of Jews in medieval and Renaissance drama is that they are at fault for their benighted religion, not their ethnic identity. The Jews in the Croxton play are converted to Christianity. Medieval Christianity often portrayed Jews as types of those needing to be baptized in the true faith. Jessica in *The Merchant of Venice* joins the Christians in Belmont, at the considerable pain of alienating her father. Similarly, Abigail in *The Jew of Malta* falls in love with a Christian, becomes a nun in earnest after having pretended earlier to be a nun as part of her father's scheming, and is destroyed by her father. The issues of loyalty and belief are understandably more complex in these Renaissance plays than in medieval drama; none the less, Abigail is good-hearted, innocent, loving, and finally a victim of her father's vengefulness. Her goodness stands out in a world that is generally pitiless and corrupt—on the Christian side as much as on the Jewish. While her goodness results in her victimization, it may also serve as a point of view from which to feel anxious about the lack of charitableness in a world dominated by power-hungry men. 'I perceive there is no love on earth, / Pity in Jews, nor piety in Turks' (III.iii.53–4), she concludes, and we are obliged to agree.

The issue of Barabas's Jewishness is complicated by the suggestion that he is also a disciple of Machiavelli. Machiavel himself appears in the play's Prologue, mockingly asking the audience not to let Barabas 'be entertained the worse / Because he favours me' (ll. 34–5). Barabas's huge wealth, says Machiavel, 'was not got without my means' (l. 32). The play itself amply reinforces this impression: Barabas is cunning, ruthless, a practised deceiver, a superb actor able to play whatever role suits his purposes. The Machiavel he embodies is not the astute historian and political theorist of Florence who counselled rulers in the art of *realpolitik* and whose view of history was essentially an optimistic one of arguing that human decisiveness can materially influence the course of events. Barabas's Machiavel is instead the hated and feared (and sometimes admired) stereotype of the English imagination, the Italian atheist who saw religion and law as mere ideologies to be manipulated for political gain. 'I count religion but a childish toy', exults Machiavel in the Prologue. 'Might first made kings' (ll. 14, 20). By his endorsement of Barabas, Machiavel invites the audience to expect a protagonist who is gargantuan and protean in his villainy.

Nor does Barabas disappoint these expectations. A major part of his appeal as a theatrical figure is that he is so endlessly resourceful in his machinations. He dominates the stage; he co-opts us as accessories to his various crimes with his candidly humorous asides; he compels admiration for his cleverness and determination. He seems larger than life, so much so that his biography seems implausibly composite. He has amassed an epic fortune in the face of great odds, and, when stripped of his wealth by the Governor of Malta, has bounced right back again. He tells Ithamore that in his youth he studied medicine, mainly in order to learn the art of poisoning. He then became an 'engineer' or deviser of ingenious military hardware, catering to both sides 'in the wars 'twixt France and Germany'. After that he was a usurer and con artist, responsible for causing so much human unhappiness with his foreclosures that he has 'filled the jails with bankrupts in a year' and created an endless demand for orphanages (II.iii.177–203). Ithamore's career is similarly generic. Barabas and Ithamore are drawn to each other by a purity of hatred and a love of villainy that are timelessly independent of the particular conflicts Barabas encounters at the hands of the Maltese authorities. As he says to Ithamore: 'Make account of me / As of thy fellow; we are villains both; / Both circumcisèd, we hate Christians both' (ll. 216–18).

The gloating villainy of these two reminds us of the Vice in many a morality play, whose devil-inspired antics had long demonstrated to English audiences how evil could be immensely funny and entertaining. *The Jew of Malta* is close to a number of Elizabethan morality plays like *The Longer Thou Livest the More Fool Thou Art* and *Enough Is as Good as a Feast* (*c.* 1559–70), in which diabolical evil is specifically linked to usury and other grasping ways of exploiting the marketplace.

At the same time, Barabas plays on our sympathies as a member of a persecuted minority. Like Shylock in Shakespeare's *The Merchant of Venice*, Barabas is both malicious and the victim of unsparing enemies. When Ferneze, the Governor of Malta, imposes a severe tax on the Jews of Malta as aliens and then refuses to allow Barabas to recant and pay the tax after his first vehement denial, Barabas is given some potent rhetoric of righteous indignation:

> What? Bring you scripture to confirm your wrongs?
> Preach me not out of my possessions.
> Some Jews are wicked, as all Christians are;
> But say the tribe that I descended of
> Were all in general cast away for sin,
> Shall I be tried by their transgression?
> The man that dealeth righteously shall live;
> And which of you can charge me otherwise?   (I.ii.111–18)

Barabas is objecting not so much to the ruinous tax itself as to the sanctimonious way in which he is being presumed guilty through the 'inherent sin' of the 'first curse' that he purportedly has inherited as a Jew—the Jews having cried out at Christ's crucifixion, 'His blood be on us, and on our children' (Matthew, 27.25).

Marlowe exploits to their limit these potent issues of decency and toleration. Like Shakespeare, he forces his audiences to examine matters of conscience and fair play. Yet Marlowe also undercuts this impression with a theatrical tour de force by suggesting, at the end of Act I scene ii, that Barabas has been playing the role of victim for all it is worth. His outraged cries against the 'unrelenting flinty hearts' and 'stony breasts' of his Christian persecutors, and his lamenting the 'sorrow for this sudden chance' that has prompted him to speak 'in the trouble of my spirit' (ll. 142–3, 207–8), give way in soliloquy to a matter-of-fact examination of the options that are still open to a person of his 'cunning'. 'Evils are apt to happen every day', he notes (ll. 225).

More tellingly, Barabas despises his fellow Jews for being so credulous and spineless as to accept their fate with resignation. Earlier, he has not been at all candid with them in his assessment of the dangers threatening the Jews of Malta. He seems to have no sense of community with them, for all his talk of being a Jewish merchant like other Jewish merchants. He tells us in soliloquy that he will not be distressed if the Turks *combat, conquer, and kill all, / So they spare me, my daughter, and my wealth* (I.i.151–2). His sole regard is for Abigail, and yet he is perfectly willing to bring about the death of Abigail's beloved, Mathias, as part of his scheme to get back at Ferneze. When Abigail turns away from her father, bitterly noting that he has destroyed Mathias even though the young man 'ne'er offended thee' (III.iii.47), even she becomes an object of Barabas's ingenious revenge. Barabas's motto is to look out for Number One: '*Ego mihimet sum semper proximus*' (I.i.188).

Barabas's misanthropy could be explained as a bitter response to persecution, and indeed part of his fascination as a character is that the human element is always present. Even so, the dramatic impression of him is increasingly of one who conspires for the sake of intrigue and devilry. In part, this growing sense of his villainy comes about through Barabas's increasing association with Ithamore, and, through Ithamore, with the grossly comic characters who people many of the play's later scenes. Barabas's cleverness is tested to the limit in his dealings with a whore named Bellamira and her thieving pimp, Pilia-Borza, who see an opportunity to blackmail Barabas. Even when Barabas copes with more serious political rivals in Act V, we see him playing off the Turks against Ferneze in a razzle-dazzle of counter-espionage and double-dealing that makes for great theatre but also turns Barabas into something of a darkly comic figure. His demise is, for that reason, less tragic in nature than grotesquely comic: we see the roof falling in on a manipulative villain, one who has filled the stage with his inventive energy but who also has eventually met his match in a manipulator who is more clever than he.

The ending seems, on first consideration, to restore some idea of order on Malta. The complexity of our response at the end, however, owes much to our evaluation of Ferneze, the Governor of the island. Ferneze is the nemesis figure who brings Barabas to justice for many murders, including that of Lodowick (the Governor's own son), Mathias, Abigail, the nuns, the friars, and still more. Yet Ferneze arguably gave Barabas cause at the start of the play by his seemingly arbitrary imposition of the tax and his refusal to allow Barabas to reconsider. Ferneze's Christian sanctimoniousness in tracking down a villain who is, arguably, no more reprehensible than his accuser and judge provides the occasion for Barabas's most poignant defence of his dignity as a human being. *The Jew of Malta* is, in these terms, a play in which might makes right and then goes about to justify itself with the pieties of orthodox morality. Few endings of plays can match the irony of Ferneze's concluding couplet: 'So, march away, and let due praise be given / Neither to fate nor fortune, but to heaven'. Ferneze strikes us pre-eminently as a ruler who knows how to invoke such moral truisms for his own political ends.

Do these convenient hypocrisies make Ferneze a reprehensible figure? Perhaps the most intriguingly subversive reading of *The Jew of Malta* we can entertain is to suppose that Ferneze is the play's hero, after all, and that he is a genuine Machiavellian in a play where the Machiavelli of stage and imagination is subjected to a range of conflicting attitudes. Ferneze uses religious orthodoxy as a bulwark of the state, and is seemingly not troubled by any hypocrisy that may hover about his invocations of the Deity. His chief concern is the survival of Malta, which is to say, the survival of his own rule as Malta's Governor.

In his dealings with the Turks and Spanish, Ferneze is as ruthless and cunning as the ruler of a small island in the Mediterranean needs to be. He pays tribute to the Turks when he cannot afford to do otherwise, and, when he needs money to pay that tribute, he levies it among an alien population whose political support he can most easily afford to alienate. His Christian subjects and advisers support his tax of the Jews, on the grounds that the Jews have prospered on Malta and can help to pay for its defence. Indeed, Ferneze seems to be a popular and successful ruler. He is not corrupt in the ordinary sense, so far as we know, of taking bribes or countenancing venery in his subordinates. He moves swiftly to punish offenders. When the Spanish admiral Del Bosco offers military support in return for Ferneze's breaking the treaty with the Turkish Calymath, Ferneze does so gladly; the Spanish are Christians, after all, and appear to be more powerful in his end of the Mediterranean. Ferneze's various gambits pay off. At the last he has both avenged his son and regained power on the island that he evidently believes to be providentially his. Religion is not just a show for him, however convenient its pieties may be.

Perhaps, then, Ferneze is Marlowe's admired man of destiny, rewarded for his canniness in a play that simultaneously demonizes 'Machiavellism' in its popularly perceived caricature. The play appears to reward virtue and punish vice in a play for the London popular stage while at the same time undercutting and complicating what is meant by 'virtue'. (The word, after all, meant 'power' in a root sense; *virtu* was a trade name for the Machiavellian.) Marlowe as a dramatist and poet gives every indication of having been exhilarated by such a matter-of-fact view of human history, and the play's huge success attests to the receptivity of Marlowe's audience. Londoners no doubt felt a whole spectrum of responses to the idea of Machiavelli (whom they were not allowed to read in English translation) from hysterical hatred to admiration. *The Jew of Malta* gave opportunity for widely varying and even contradictory responses. Here, as in Marlowe's other plays, like *Tamburlaine*, London audiences could resonate to the heady prospect of a world in which political conflicts are determined by force and guile, in which most Christians are no better than most Jews or pagans, in which the representatives of organized religion are both venal and lecherous, and in which the sheer force of personal magnetism can change history—for good or evil.

RECENT CRITICAL TRENDS

The Jew of Malta is available in a number of good modern editions. Although the original text is problematic to some scholars because of its purported unevenness of tone, it exists in a single authoritative early quarto and has been faithfully followed by most of its editors. Standard old spelling editions of Marlowe's dramatic works include those of Fredson Bowers, C. F. Tucker Brooke, and Roma Gill.[1] Modern spelling editions of the works include those of David Bevington and Eric Rasmussen; R. H. Case; Roma Gill; Leo Kirschbaum; Irving Ribner; E. D. Pendry and J. C. Maxwell; M. R. Ridley; and J. B. Steane.[2] *The Jew of Malta* is included in all these editions. For individual editions of this play alone, see T. W. Craik, N. W. Bawcutt, Irving Ribner, and Richard Van Fossen.[3] Two concordances are available: that of Robert J. Fehrenbach *et al.* keyed to the Bowers text, and that of Louis Ule, with modernized spellings for its entries and modern- and old-spelling texts in parallel columns.[4]

The Jew of Malta was not a favourite among traditional scholars in the nineteenth and early twentieth centuries. John Bakeless, in his *The Tragical History of Christopher Marlowe* (1942), is perhaps typical in condemning it as not even a good play, because it breaks in the middle, descending from tragic grandeur into chicanery.[5] T. S. Eliot ranks among the first, in *The Sacred Wood* (1960), to defend the play by arguing that it does indeed have coherence: it is a 'farce of the Old English humor, the terribly serious, even savage, comic humor'.[6] This line of defence has been vociferously seconded by recent criticism. Wilbur Sanders, for example, in *The Dramatist and the Received Idea* (1968), interprets the play as 'a courageous attack on a powerful and particularly vicious social prejudice'.[7] The question of genre becomes vital. Is the play a tragedy or a black comedy of satire? Clifford Leech studies the problem as one of paradox in *Christopher Marlowe: Poet for the Stage*, by asking, 'Black Comedy or Comic Tragedy?'[8] To Douglas Cole (*Suffering and Evil in the Plays of Christopher Marlowe*), the play needs to be understood as 'a spectacle of personified evil at work, rather than a spectacle of tragic suffering'.[9] To force certain generic expectations on the play is to require that it conform to irrelevant classical standards.

A major strength of the play, in the view of those who have remedied its beleaguered nineteenth-century reputation, lies in its unsparing honesty of criticism directed at a corrupt social and political order, together with its wry portrayal of human aspiration. Una Ellis-Fermor deserves major credit, in her early *Christopher Marlowe* (1927), for seeing the play as 'another expression of the aspiration, of the longing to outstrip man's limitation, that he [Marlowe] had first revealed in *Tamburlaine*'. In *The Jew of Malta*, argues Ellis-Fermor, Marlowe combines 'the aspiring soul of man' with 'his desire to exceed his mortal nature'. The play is not, like *Tamburlaine*, the enshrinement of a dream, nor, like *Doctor Faustus*, the tragedy of an isolated thinker, but is instead 'the picture of the Elizabethan world of "policy", in which men were unscrupulous, bold, implacable, cruel in power and sometimes heroic in defeat'.[10] Harry Levin's *The Overreacher* takes a similar view: Barabas is the continuation of Marlowe's study of *libido dominandi*, the lust for power; it employs conspiracy rather than, as in *Tamburlaine*, conquest —'policy rather than prowess'. Gold is to Barabas what power is to Tamburlaine.[11] Paul Kocher's *Christopher Marlowe* studies the play as a clash of abstract creeds, setting Judaism and Christianity against each other 'in such a way as to equalize the two' on moral as well as ideological grounds.[12]

The colossal dominance of Barabas's evil has prompted a number of investigations of his character in terms of sources and motive. Bernard Spivack (*Shakespeare and the Allegory of Evil*) argues that Barabas is a Vice figure in the tradition of the morality play, and as such is an anticipation of Shakespeare's Richard III, Iago, and Edmund. Like the Vice, Barabas gloats to the audience, shows off the sheer versatility of his machinations, and manipulates the lives of other characters, acting all the while out of purely evil and diabolical intent.[13] David Bevington, taking up this issue in *From 'Mankind' to Marlowe*, demonstrates how Barabas operates as a Vice in a play that is constructed throughout on dramaturgic principles of linear sequencing and of rapid alternation between scenes of high seriousness and comic villainy; the restlessness of Barabas's character stems from the unresolved way in which he is compounded of historically plausible elements and more timelessly metaphysical aspects derived from the morality play.[14] Constance Brown Kurjyama takes a more psychological approach in *Hammer or Anvil*, arguing that Barabas's seemingly gratuitous motives for violent evil are fully explicable when we look at him in terms of an archaic, pregenital, anal, compensatory aggression aimed at self-preservation and the bolstering of self-esteem, as the main character confronts a world in which one either exploits or is exploited.[15]

The dog-eat-dog aura of Malta and the Mediterranean world offers itself as rich material for New Historicist critics. Stephen Greenblatt's chapter on Marlowe in Renaissance *Self-Fashioning* (1980) looks at Marlowe's protagonists, including Barabas, as acquisitive entrepreneurs whose alienated restlessness drives them towards compulsive, repetitive acts of self-assertion and self-definition.[16] William Zunder's *Marlowe* similarly sees Barabas as a merchant capitalist.[17] Barabas as Outsider prompts examination of his Jewishness, as for example in Greenblatt's 'Marlowe, Marx, and Anti-Semitism', arguing that Marlowe, when compared with Marx, can be seen as more committed to an 'anarchic discharge of energy' than to any hoped-for emancipation of the underdog.[18] Yet the figure of the persecuted Jew as Other does command at least a fitful sympathy; see Lloyd Kermode's essay on 'Marlowe's Second City'.[19] Emily Bartels studies colonialism in 'Malta, the Jew, and the Fictions of Difference', concluding that Malta is an object of colonialist discourse throughout the play and that the Spanish Del Bosco comes to represent 'the colonizing voice behind the colonizing voice' of Ferneze.[20]

Ferneze is an object of fascination among those critics interested in political analysis. He is, as Catherine Minshull sees him and as the present Introduction argues, the only true devotee of Machiavelli's writings in a play dominated by Barabas as a practitioner of the prevailing caricature of Machiavellism as pure atheist amorality.[21] As a number of critics have shown, the stage Machiavel of the play owes much to the popular image of Machiavelli as derived from Gentillet.[22] Simon Shepherd (*Marlowe and the Politics of Elizabethan*

Theatre) takes a 'socialist and anti-patriarchal' approach to the play's politics as a way of showing how Marlowe's rhetorical methods are deeply revelatory of the discourse of power relations.[23] Claude Summers (*Christopher Marlowe and the Politics of Power*) sees the play as one in which the principle of *virtú* operates to bitter and universal effect.[24]

Feminist discourse, no less interested in the play's Otherness, is especially attracted to Abigail. A case in point is Jeremy Tambling's 'Abigail's Party: "The Difference of Things" in *The Jew of Malta*', showing how Abigail, in terms of the play's structure, is to be seen as 'an object, displaced by the gold she showers on her father'. In a world of male power, narcissism, and male bonding, Abigail offers a radical alternative, but one that can pose only a weakened challenge to the play's antifeminist premises; her death is not the climax of the play, but only part of a 'half-comic crescendo of villainy'.[25] She is, as Michel Poirier shows, a character wholly invented by Marlowe, and is thus a tribute to his power of invention.[26]

Major points of contact between *The Jew of Malta* and Shakespeare's *The Merchant of Venice* (written in part, it seems, as a response to a revival of *The Jew of Malta* in 1594) invite considerations of these two plays in comparative terms. One notable such undertaking is James Shapiro's *Rival Playwrights*, in which questions of influence are posed in the fruitful context of Harold Bloom's seminal work, *The Anxiety of Influence*.[27] Maurice Charney similarly undertakes to show, in 'Jessica's Turquoise Ring and Abigail's Poisoned Porridge', how Shakespeare nervously undertook to go beyond the work of his famous predecessor and rival by writing 'in a less heroic and more complex mode'.[28]

Growing interest in Marlowe has produced a recent collection of essays: '*A Poet and a Filthy Play-maker: New Essays on Christopher Marlowe*.[29] It contains three essays on *The Jew of Malta*. Thomas Cartelli's 'Endless Play' sees a theatrical mode 'that encourages and facilitates the informal interplay of fantasy instead of the formal imitation of an action, that communicates a sense of shared make-believe without ever really requiring our willing suspension of disbelief'. Edward Rocklin, in 'Marlowe as Experimental Dramatist', explores Marlowe's innovative use of inherited dramaturgy in *The Jew of Malta*; the prologue spoken by Machiavelli establishes 'both the play's framing question and the role of the audience'. Barabas seems not only to generate the action but 'to maintain control of the audience's perspective on that action'. Coburn Freer ('Lies and

Lying in *The Jew of Malta*') looks at ways in which Barabas 'consistently collapses the distinction between social fictions and lies'.

Other studies show a similar interest in dramaturgic techniques and in audience response. F. P. Wilson has some perceptive things to say about dramaturgy in *Marlowe and the Early Shakespeare*.[30] Judith Weil's *Christopher Marlowe: Merlin's Prophet* looks at Marlowe in terms of subtle rhetorical manipulation aimed at confronting the audience with a conflicting sense of a protagonist who is morally flawed and yet passionately energetic and fascinating.[31] Bruce Edwin Brandt's *Christopher Marlowe and the Metaphysical Problem Play* focuses on the radically unsettling effects of specific metaphysical premises in conflict with the protagonist's aspirations.[32] Recent criticism thus seems more interested in social commentary and dramatic technique than in the older questions, now largely forgotten, of the play's ethical worth and its genre.

Further research on *The Jew of Malta* can be facilitated by several bibliographies: those of Robert Kimbrough (1973), Irving Ribner and Clifford Chalmers Huffman (1978), Lois Mai Chan with Sarah A. Pederson (1978), Kenneth Friedenreich (1979), and Ronald Levao (1988), updating Jonathan Post (1977).[33]

NOTES

1 Fredson Bowers, ed., *The Complete Works of Christopher Marlowe*, 2 vols. (Cambridge, 1973); C. F. Tucker Brooke, ed., *The Works of Christopher Marlowe* (Oxford, 1910, rpt. 1966), and Roma Gill, ed., *The Complete Works of Christopher Marlowe*, 3 vols. (Oxford, c. 1990).

2 David Bevington and Eric Rasmussen, eds, *Four Plays of Marlowe* (Oxford, 1995); R. H. Case, ed., *The Works and Life of Christopher Marlowe*, 6 vols. (1930–33); Roma Gill, *The Plays of Christopher Marlowe* (Oxford, 1971); Leo Kirschbaum, ed., *The Plays of Christopher Marlowe* (Cleveland, 1962); Irving Ribner, *The Complete Plays of Christopher Marlowe* (New York, 1963); E. D. Pendry and J. C. Maxwell, eds, *Christopher Marlowe: Complete Plays and Poems* (London, 1976); M. R. Ridley, ed., *Christopher Marlowe: Plays and Poems* (London, 1955), and J. B. Steane, ed., *The Complete Plays of Christopher Marlowe* (Baltimore, 1969).

3 T. W. Craik, ed., *The Jew of Malta* (London, 1966); N. W. Bawcutt, ed., *The Jew of Malta* (Manchester, 1978); Irving Ribner, ed., *The Jew of Malta* (New York, 1970), and Richard Van Fossen, ed., *The Jew of Malta* (Lincoln, Nebraska, 1964).

4 Robert J. Fehrenbach, Lea Ann Boone, and Mario A. DiCesare, eds, *A Concordance to the Plays, Poems, and Translations of Christopher Marlowe*

(1982), and Louis Ule, *A Concordance to the Works of Christopher Marlowe* (1979).

5 John Bakeless, *The Tragicall History of Christopher Marlowe* Cambridge, Ma., 1942).

6 T. S. Eliot, 'Notes on the Blank Verse of Christopher Marlowe' in *The Sacred Wood* (London, 1960), p. 92. The essay was written some time earlier.

7 Wilbur Sanders, *The Dramatist and the Received Idea: Studies in the Plays of Marlowe and Shakespeare* (London, 1968), p. 288.

8 Clifford Leech, '*The Jew of Malta*: Black Comedy or Comic Tragedy?' in *Christopher Marlowe: Poet for the Stage* (New York, 1986), pp. 159–74.

9 Douglas Cole, *Suffering and Evil in the Plays of Christopher Marlowe* (Princeton, 1962), p. 123.

10 Una Ellis-Fermor, *Christopher Marlowe* (London, 1927).

11 Harry Levin, *The Overreacher: A Study of Christopher Marlowe* (Cambridge, Ma., 1952).

12 Paul H. Kocher, *Christopher Marlowe: A Study of His Thought, Learning, and Character* (Chapel Hill, N.C., 1946).

13 Bernard Spivack, *Shakespeare and the Allegory of Evil* (New York, 1958).

14 David Bevington, *From 'Mankind' to Marlowe: Growth of Structure in the Popular Drama of Tudor England* (Cambridge, Ma., 1962).

15 Constance Brown Kuriyama, *Hammer or Anvil: Psychological Patterns in Christopher Marlowe's Plays* (New Brunswick, N. J., 1980).

16 Stephen Greenblatt, *Renaissance Self-Fashioning: From More to Shakespeare* (Chicago, 1980).

17 William Zunder, *Marlowe* (Cottingham, Hull, 1994).

18 Stephen Greenblatt, 'Marlowe, Marx, and Anti-Semitism', *Critical Inquiry*, 5 (1978), 291–307.

19 Lloyd Edward Kermode, ' "Marlowe's Second City": The Jew as Critic at the Rose in 1592', *SEL*, 35.2 (1995), 215–29.

20 Emily C. Bartels, 'Malta, the Jew, and the Fictions of Difference: Colonialist Discourse in Marlowe's *The Jew of Malta*', *ELR*, 20 (1990), 1–16.

21 Catherine Minshull, 'Marlowe's "Sound Machevill" ', *RenD*, 13 (1982), 35–53.

22 See Irving Ribner, 'Marlowe and Machiavelli', *Comparative Literature*, 6 (1954), 348–56, and A. L. Rowse, *Christopher Marlowe: His Life and Work* (New York, 1964), pp. 81–100.

23 Simon Shepherd, *Marlowe and the Politics of Elizabethan Theatre* (1986).

24 Claude J. Summers, *Christopher Marlowe and the Politics of Power* (Salzburg, 1974).

25 Jeremy Tambling, 'Abigail's Party: "The Difference of Things" in *The Jew of Malta*' in *In Another Country: Feminist Perspectives on Renaissance*

Drama, ed. Dorothea Kehler and Susan Baker (Metuchen, N. J., 1991), pp. 95–112.

26 Michel Poirier, *Christopher Marlowe* (London, 1951).

27 James Shapiro, *Rival Playwrights: Marlowe, Jonson, and Shakespeare* (New York, 1991).

28 Maurice Charney, 'Jessica's Turquoise Ring and Abigail's Poisoned Porridge: Shakespeare and Marlowe as Rivals and Imitators', *RenD*, 10 (1979), 33–44.

29 Kenneth Friedenreich, Roma Gill, and Constance B. Kuriyama, eds, '*A Poet and a Filthy Play-maker*': *New Essays on Christopher Marlowe* (New York, 1988).

30 F. P. Wilson, *Marlowe and the Early Shakespeare* (Oxford, 1953), pp. 57–68.

31 Judith E. R. Weil, *Christopher Marlowe: Merlin's Prophet* (Cambridge, 1977).

32 Bruce Edwin Brandt, *Christopher Marlowe and the Metaphysical Problem Play* (Salzburg, 1985).

33 Robert Kimbrough, 'Recent Studies in Marlowe', in *Recent Studies in English Renaissance Drama*, ed. Terence P. Logan and Denzel A. Smith, 4 vols. (1973); Irving Ribner and Clifford Chalmers Huffman, *Tudor and Stuart Drama* (Goldentree Bibliographies, 1978); Lois Mai Chan with Sarah A. Pederson, *Marlowe Criticism: A Bibliography* (Boston, 1978); Kenneth Friedenreich, *Christopher Marlowe: An Annotated Bibliography of Criticism Since 1950* (Metuchen, N. J., 1979), and Ronald Levao, 'Recent Studies in Marlowe (1977–1986)', *ELR*, 18 (1988), 329–42, updating Jonathan F. S. Post, 'Recent Studies in Marlowe (1968–1976)', *ELR*, 7 (1977), 382–99.

THE
JEW OF MALTA

[DRAMATIS PERSONAE

MACHIAVEL, *speaker of the Prologue.*
BARABAS, *the Jew of Malta.*
ITHAMORE, *slave to Barabas.*
ABIGAIL, *Barabas's daughter.*
FERNEZE, *the Governor of Malta.*
SELIM CALYMATH, *son of the Emperor of Turkey.*
MARTIN DEL BOSCO, *Vice-Admiral of Spain.*
DON LODOWICK, *the Governor's son.*
DON MATHIAS, *his friend.*
KATHERINE, *Mother of Mathias.*
FRIAR JACOMO.
FRIAR BERNARDINE.
Abbess.
BELLAMIRA, *a Courtesan.*
PILIA-BORZA, *a thief, in league with Bellamira.*
Two Merchants; Three Jews; Knights of Malta; a Nun;
    Bashaws, Officers, Slaves, Citizens of Malta, Turkish
    soldiers (Janizaries), Messenger, Carpenters.

The Scene: *Malta.*]

The Jew of Malta

[Prologue]

[Enter] MACHIAVEL.

Machiavel. Albeit the world think Machiavel is dead,
    Yet was his soul but flown beyond the Alps,
    And, now the Guise is dead, is come from France
    To view this land and frolic with his friends.
    To some perhaps my name is odious,   5
    But such as love me guard me from their tongues;
    And let them know that I am Machiavel,
    And weigh not men, and therefore not men's words.
    Admired I am of those that hate me most.
    Though some speak openly against my books,   10
    Yet will they read me and thereby attain

Prol. 1. *Machiavel*] Niccolò Machiavelli (1469–1527), the famous Italian philosopher, author of *The Prince* and *Discourses on the First Ten Books of Livy*, among other works, was a hated name to many English persons (who could have read him in Italian, French, or Latin, though no English translation was available) because his presumed espousal of *realpolitik* was widely seen as godless and amoral. Marlowe evokes the legendary Machiavelli, not the historical figure.

2. *beyond the Alps*] i.e. from Italy into France and thence to England.

3. *the Guise*] Henry, third Duke of Guise, was assassinated on 23 December 1588 by order of the French king Henry III, an event dramatized by Marlowe himself in scene xxi of *The Massacre at Paris*. Guise was a bitter enemy of the French Protestants, or Huguenots, who regarded him as evil and ambitious, since he was the chief architect of the slaughter of many Huguenots at the Massacre at St Bartholomew in 1572. The association with Machiavelli seems to have been Marlowe's invention.

4. *this land*] England (even though the play is set in Malta).

6.] 'But those who are my true followers refrain from naming me openly (lest those who hate me be alarmed).'

7. *them*] i.e. my true followers; or, my detractors.

8. *weigh not*] attach no value to, am not impressed by. Machiavel has no respect for conventional pieties.

17

To Peter's chair, and, when they cast me off,
Are poisoned by my climbing followers.
I count religion but a childish toy,
And hold there is no sin but ignorance.   15
Birds of the air will tell of murders past?
I am ashamed to hear such fooleries!
Many will talk of title to a crown;
What right had Caesar to the empery?
Might first made kings, and laws were then most sure   20
When like the Draco's they were writ in blood.
Hence comes it that a strong-built citadel
Commands much more than letters can import—
Which maxima had Phalaris observed,
He'd never bellowed in a brazen bull   25

---

12. *Peter's chair*] i.e. the papacy. Machiavel boasts that clerics who aspire to the papacy secretly use his methods of intrigue, and, when they then adopt a more pious pose as pope, are overthrown by other closet Machiavellians. Marlowe plays upon English suspicion and hatred of the papacy as ruled by guile, deceit, and worldly insolence.

15. *ignorance*] either (1) ignorance of the rules for worldly success, or (2) the kind of superstition jeered at in ll. 16–17.

16.] Plutarch, in his *Moralia*, tells of cranes which revealed the murder of Ibycus. Machiavel ridicules the notion that God's providence might be discovered by such means.

19. *empery*] empire, rule, dominion. Machiavel here claims Julius Caesar as a follower because Caesar seized power by force. The historical Machiavelli, in his *Discourses*, described Caesar as a tyrant, in the tradition of Lucan's *Pharsalia*.

20. *Might . . . kings*] Machiavel here echoes Jean Bodin, implicitly rejecting both the theory that royal power came about through a voluntary surrender of authority by the community to a person most fit to rule and the pious theory that royal power was providentially ordained.

21. *Draco*] an Athenian legislator who received in 621 B.C. special authority to codify and promulgate laws for the city, replacing private vengeance with a code that became proverbial for its severity.

23. *letters*] erudition.

24. *maxima*] maxim. (The quarto reads 'maxime'.)

Phalaris] tyrant of Acragas in Sicily in the sixth century B.C. who is reported to have roasted his victims in a brazen bull invented by Perillus, and to have put Perillus himself to death as the bull's first victim. Machiavel appears to follow an account in Ovid's *Ibis* describing how Phalaris too died in the bull. Phalaris was allowed by Erasmus to have one redeeming feature, his love of letters; to Machiavel, this is his fatal weakness.

Of great ones' envy. O' the poor petty wights
Let me be envied and not pitièd!
But whither am I bound? I come not, I,
To read a lecture here in Britany,
But to present the tragedy of a Jew,   30
Who smiles to see how full his bags are crammed,
Which money was not got without my means.
I crave but this: grace him as he deserves,
And let him not be entertained the worse
Because he favours me.   35

[*Exit.*]

---

26. *Of . . . envy*] Machiavel may refer to an uprising among the aristocrats and people of Agrigentum that led to Phalaris' downfall, or else conflates the stories of Phalaris and Perillus in such a way as to reflect Perillus' outcry against his fate.

petty wights] commoners of no importance. Machiavel would rather be envied for his cunning than pitied as a loser, just as he thinks Phalaris would have been better off tending to his strong citadel rather than striving for a humane reputation as a man of letters. (In fact, the so-called *Letters of Phalaris* have been shown to be spurious.) Q's *wites* can be read as 'wights' or as 'wits'.

28. *whither . . . bound*] i.e. 'Where am I going?' Machiavel has let his tongue run away with him.

29. *read*] give.

Britany] Britain; a form widely used in Elizabethan English.

33. *grace*] show favour to.

34. *entertained*] received, accepted.

35. *favours me*] (1) takes my part; (2) resembles me.

Act I

Enter BARABAS *in his counting-house,*
with heaps of gold before him.

Barabas. So that of thus much that return was made,
And, of the third part of the Persian ships,
There was the venture summed and satisfied.
As for those Samnites and the men of Uz
That bought my Spanish oils and wines of Greece,   5
Here have I pursed their paltry silverlings.
Fie, what a trouble 'tis to count this trash!
Well fare the Arabians, who so richly pay
The things they traffic for with wedge of gold,
Whereof a man may easily in a day   10
Tell that which may maintain him all his life.

I.i.0.1–2.] As he exits, Machiavel may draw back a curtain in front of a
'discovery space' revealing Barabas at his counting table. The actor presumably comes forward to be better seen and heard. Barabas's name is that of the
murderer (Matthew, 27.16–26, Mark, 15.7, Luke, 23.18) and robber (John,
18.40) whom the Jews ask Pilate to release to them rather than Christ. In
patristic tradition he became a type of Antichrist. His name throughout is
stressed on the first syllable and, less emphatically, the last.

1–3.] 'So that in return for such-and-such an investment in shipping I've
earned this much profit; my actual costs amount to only one-third of my
overall worth in Persian shipping.'

3. *summed and satisfied*] reckoned up and paid off. Barabas, having tripled
his investment, has easily paid off the capital.

4. *Samnites*] a central Italian tribe conquered by the Romans, after a long
struggle, in 295 B.C. The word is only a guess at Q's *Samintes*.

Uz] a biblical land referred to in Job, 1.1.

6. *silverlings*] used in early sixteenth-century translations of the Bible as an
equivalent for the shekel, a Jewish coin (and less valuable than gold).

8. *Well . . . Arabians*] either (1) may the Arabians prosper! or (2) the
Arabians thrive.

9. *traffic*] carry on trade.

11. *Tell*] reckon up. (Compare *telling* in l. 16.)

The needy groom that never fingered groat
Would make a miracle of thus much coin;
But he whose steel-barred coffers are crammed full,
And all his lifetime hath been tired,   15
Wearying his fingers' ends with telling it,
Would in his age be loath to labour so,
And for a pound to sweat himself to death.
Give me the merchants of the Indian mines
That trade in metal of the purest mould,   20
The wealthy Moor that in the eastern rocks
Without control can pick his riches up
And in his house heap pearl like pebble-stones,
Receive them free, and sell them by the weight—
Bags of fiery opals, sapphires, amethysts,   25
Jacinths, hard topaz, grass-green emeralds,
Beauteous rubies, sparkling diamonds,
And seld-seen costly stones of so great price
As one of them, indifferently rated
And of a carat of this quantity,   30
May serve in peril of calamity
To ransom great kings from captivity.
This is the ware wherein consists my wealth;
And thus, methinks, should men of judgement frame
Their means of traffic from the vulgar trade,   35
And, as their wealth increaseth, so enclose
Infinite riches in a little room.
But now, how stands the wind?
Into what corner peers my halcyon's bill?

---

12. *groat*] a small silver coin worth fourpence.
13. *make . . . of*] think it miraculous to behold.
21. *the eastern rocks*] probably the Arabian desert, parts of which were thought to be fabulously rich in precious stones.
22. *Without control*] freely, without restraint.
24.] 'gather the pearls at no cost and sell them by gross weight rather than individually'.
28. *seld-seen*] seldom seen, rare.
29.] 'that one such jewel, valued impartially'.
31. *in . . . calamity*] in time of crisis.
34. *frame*] arrange.
35. *from*] in a way different or quite apart from.
39. *halcyon's bill*] The body of a halcyon or kingfisher was thought to act as a weather-vane if hung up where the wind would catch it.

Ha, to the east? Yes. See how stands the vanes!   40
East and by south. Why then, I hope my ships
I sent for Egypt and the bordering isles
Are gotten up by Nilus' winding banks;
Mine argosy from Alexandria,
Loaden with spice and silks, now under sail,   45
Are smoothly gliding down by Candy shore
To Malta, through our Mediterranean Sea.

Enter a Merchant.

But who comes here? How now?
Merchant. Barabas, thy ships are safe,
Riding in Malta road; and all the merchants   50
With all their merchandise are safe arrived,
And have sent me to know whether yourself
Will come and custom them.
Barabas. The ships are safe, thou say'st, and richly fraught?
Merchant. They are.
Barabas.   Why then, go bid them come ashore   55
And bring with them their bills of entry;
I hope our credit in the custom-house
Will serve as well as I were present there.
Go send 'em threescore camels, thirty mules,
And twenty waggons to bring up the ware.   60
But art thou master in a ship of mine,
And is thy credit not enough for that?
Merchant. The very custom barely comes to more
Than many merchants of the town are worth,

---

42. *the bordering isles*] i.e. Cyprus and Crete; see l. 46.
43. *Are . . . by*] have reached.
44. *Mine argosy*] i.e. (I hope that) my fleet of large merchant ships.
45. *Loaden*] laden.
46.] 'are sailing smoothly along the shores of Crete'.
50. *road*] roadstead, harbour.
51. *all their*] Perhaps Q's 'other' is a misreading of a manuscript 'al ther' (Maxwell).
53. *custom them*] pass them through customs by paying the duty.
54. *fraught*] laden with goods.
58. *as I*] as if I.
63. *The . . . barely*] even the custom duties alone.

And therefore far exceeds my credit, sir.   65
Barabas. Go tell 'em the Jew of Malta sent thee, man.
    Tush, who amongst 'em knows not Barabas?
Merchant. I go.   [*He starts to leave.*]
Barabas. So then, there's somewhat come.—
    Sirrah, which of my ships art thou master of?   70
Merchant. Of the *Speranza*, sir.
Barabas.   And saw'st thou not
    Mine argosy at Alexandria?
    Thou couldst not come from Egypt, or by Caire,
    But at the entry there into the sea
    Where Nilus pays his tribute to the main   75
    Thou needs must sail by Alexandria.
Merchant. I neither saw them nor enquired of them.
    But this we heard some of our seamen say:
    They wondered how you durst with so much wealth
    Trust such a crazèd vessel, and so far.   80
Barabas. Tush, they are wise! I know her and her strength.
    But go, go thou thy ways; discharge thy ship,
    And bid my factor bring his loading in.
                       [*Exit* Merchant.]
    And yet I wonder at this argosy.

Enter a Second Merchant.

Second Merchant. Thine argosy from Alexandria,   85
    Know, Barabas, doth ride in Malta road,
    Laden with riches and exceeding store
    Of Persian silks, of gold, and orient pearl.

69.] 'Well, at least some of my shipping has arrived safely.'
70. *Sirrah*] term of address to an inferior.
71. Speranza] The name of Barabas's ship means 'hope' in Italian.
73. *Caire*] Cairo.
75.] i.e. 'where the Nile flows into the Mediterranean'.
80. *crazèd*] unsound, not seaworthy.
81. *they are wise*] sarcastic: 'they think they know a lot about it'.
82. *go thou thy ways*] get moving.
83.] 'and bid my commercial agent bring me his bill of lading'.
84. *at*] about.
88. *orient*] lustrous, precious (as generally of jewels from the East).

Barabas. How chance you came not with those other ships
    That sailed by Egypt?
Second Merchant.   Sir, we saw 'em not.   90
Barabas. Belike they coasted round by Candy shore
    About their oils or other businesses.
    But 'twas ill done of you to come so far
    Without the aid or conduct of their ships.
Second Merchant. Sir, we were wafted by a Spanish fleet   95
    That never left us till within a league,
    That had the galleys of the Turk in chase.
Barabas. Oh, they were going up to Sicily. Well, go,
    And bid the merchants and my men dispatch
    And come ashore, and see the fraught discharged.   100
Second Merchant. I go.   *Exit.*
Barabas. Thus trolls our fortune in by land and sea,
    And thus are we on every side enriched.
    These are the blessings promised to the Jews,
    And herein was old Abram's happiness.   105
    What more may heaven do for earthly men
    Than thus to pour out plenty in their laps,
    Ripping the bowels of the earth for them,
    Making the sea their servant and the winds
    To drive their substance with successful blasts?   110
    Who hateth me but for my happiness?
    Or who is honoured now but for his wealth?

---

89. *How chance*] how does it come about that.
91. *Belike*] perchance.
92. *About their oils*] fetching a cargo of olive oil.
94. *conduct*] protective escort.
95. *wafted*] escorted, convoyed.
96. *within a league*] i.e. within three miles or so of our destination.
97.] i.e. '(we were being escorted by a Spanish fleet) that was in pursuit of the Turkish fleet'.
98. *Oh . . . Sicily*] 'Oh, the Spanish fleet was no doubt on its way to Sicily (in pursuit of the Turks).'
102. *trolls*] comes 'rolling in' abundantly.
105. *old Abram's happiness*] i.e. the covenent made between God and Abraham, giving Canaan to Abraham and his heirs for ever (Genesis, 15.13–21, 17.1–22; see also Exodus, 6.1–8, and Galatians, 3.16).
110.] 'to propel their richly laden merchant ships with propitious winds'.
111. *happiness*] good fortune, prosperity.

Rather had I, a Jew, be hated thus
Than pitied in a Christian poverty.
For I can see no fruits in all their faith   115
But malice, falsehood, and excessive pride,
Which methinks fits not their profession.
Haply some hapless man hath conscience,
And for his conscience lives in beggary.
They say we are a scattered nation;   120
I cannot tell, but we have scambled up
More wealth by far than those that brag of faith.
There's Kirriah Jairim, the great Jew of Greece,
Obed in Bairseth, Nones in Portugal,
Myself in Malta, some in Italy,   125
Many in France, and wealthy every one—
Ay, wealthier far than any Christian.
I must confess we come not to be kings.
That's not our fault. Alas, our number's few,
And crowns come either by succession   130
Or urged by force; and nothing violent,
Oft have I heard tell, can be permanent.
Give us a peaceful rule; make Christians kings,
That thirst so much for principality.
I have no charge, nor many children,   135

---

117. *profession*] professed religious faith. (Pronounced in four syllables.)

118. *hapless*] unfortunate (playing on *Haply*, perchance). The man who chooses to live by his conscience, says Barabas, will live in beggary.

121. *I cannot tell*] I cannot say as to that.

scambled up] scraped together, struggled indecorously or rapaciously in order to amass wealth.

123. *Kirriah Jairim*] a city name ('Kiraith-iearim'), cited in Joshua, 15.9 and 60, and Judges, 18.12, perhaps mistakenly given to a person in 1 Chronicles, 2.50–3, Geneva version.

124. *Obed*] a not uncommon biblical name (1 Chronicles, 2.12; Ruth, 4.17–22).

Bairseth] not identified; possibly a distortion of a biblical name such as Baaseiah (1 Chronicles, 6.40).

Nones] Some figures bearing similar names were Portuguese maranos, or Christian converts, living in Constantinople and also in London, in the mid sixteenth century.

128. *come not to be*] do not succeed in becoming.

134. *principality*] sovereignty, supreme authority.

135. *charge*] financial burden.

But one sole daughter, whom I hold as dear
As Agamemnon did his Iphigen;
And all I have is hers. But who comes here?

Enter three Jews [*speaking to one another*].

First Jew. Tush, tell not me, 'twas done of policy.
Second Jew. Come therefore, let us go to Barabas,   140
    For he can counsel best in these affairs;
    And here he comes.
Barabas.   Why, how now, countrymen?
    Why flock you thus to me in multitudes?
    What accident's betided to the Jews?
First Jew. A fleet of warlike galleys, Barabas,   145
    Are come from Turkey, and lie in our road;
    And they this day sit in the council-house
    To entertain them and their embassy.
Barabas. Why, let 'em come, so they come not to war;
    Or let 'em war, so we be conquerors.   150
    (*Aside*) *Nay, let 'em combat, conquer, and kill all,*
    So they spare me, my daughter, and my wealth.
First Jew. Were it for confirmation of a league,
    They would not come in warlike manner thus.
Second Jew. I fear their coming will afflict us all.   155
Barabas. Fond men, what dream you of their multitudes?
    What need they treat of peace that are in league?
    The Turks and those of Malta are in league.
    Tut, tut, there is some other matter in 't.
First Jew. Why, Barabas, they come for peace or war.   160
Barabas. Haply for neither, but to pass along
    Towards Venice by the Adriatic Sea,

---

137. *Agamemnon*] a dramatic irony, since Agamemnon, the leader of the Greek army in the Trojan war, was obliged to appease the goddess Artemis by sacrificing his daughter Iphigenia to her.

139. *of policy*] out of consideration for cunning statecraft. (The Jews are anxious about their being summoned to the senate-house; ll. 166–7.)

147. *they*] the Knights of Malta.

148.] 'to receive the Turkish ambassador and his retinue'.

150. *so*] provided that.

156. *Fond*] foolish, credulous.

157.] 'Why would those that already have a treaty with us need to negotiate a peace?'

With whom they have attempted many times,
But never could effect their stratagem.
Third Jew. And very wisely said; it may be so.   165
Second Jew. But there's a meeting in the senate-house,
And all the Jews in Malta must be there.
Barabas. H'm. All the Jews in Malta must be there?
Ay, like enough. Why then, let every man
Provide him and be there for fashion sake.   170
If anything shall there concern our state,
Assure yourselves I'll look—(*Aside*) *unto myself.*
First Jew. I know you will.—Well, brethren, let us go.
Second Jew. Let's take our leaves. Farewell, good Barabas.
Barabas. Do so. Farewell, Zaareth, farewell Temainte.   175
                                                    [*Exeunt* Jews.]
And, Barabas, now search this secret out.
Summon thy senses; call thy wits together.
These silly men mistake the matter clean.
Long to the Turk did Malta contribute,
Which tribute—all in policy, I fear—   180
The Turks have let increase to such a sum
As all the wealth of Malta cannot pay,
And now by that advantage thinks, belike,
To seize upon the town; ay, that he seeks.
Howe'er the world go, I'll make sure for one,   185
And seek in time to intercept the worst,
Warily guarding that which I ha' got.
'*Ego mihimet sum semper proximus.*'
Why, let 'em enter, let 'em take the town!   [*Exit.*]

---

163. *With*] against.
attempted] attacked, assaulted.
164. *effect*] bring about, accomplish.
170. *Provide him*] prepare, get himself ready.
for fashion sake] as a mere formality.
171. *state*] welfare.
178. *silly*] simple, foolish.
clean] completely.
179. *contribute*] accented on the first and third syllables.
185. *make . . . one*] look out for Number One.
186. *intercept*] anticipate, prevent.
188.] 'I am always nearest to myself', putting my own interests first.
(Ultimately from Terence, *Andria*, 4.1.12.)

[I. ii]

> *Enter* [FERNEZE,] *Governor of Malta*, Knights[, *and* Officers,]
> *met by* Bashaws *of the Turk*, [*and*] CALYMATH.

Ferneze. Now, bashaws, what demand you at our hands?
First Bashaw.
    Know, Knights of Malta, that we came from Rhodes,
    From Cyprus, Candy, and those other isles
    That lie betwixt the Mediterranean seas—
Ferneze. What's Cyprus, Candy, and those other isles   5
    To us, or Malta? What at our hands demand ye?
Calymath. The ten years' tribute that remains unpaid.
Ferneze. Alas, my lord, the sum is over-great.
    I hope your highness will consider us.
Calymath. I wish, grave governor, 'twere in my power   10
    To favour you, but 'tis my father's cause,
    Wherein I may not—nay, I dare not—dally.
Ferneze. Then give us leave, great Selim Calymath.
                [*Ferneze consults with his Knights.*]
Calymath. [*To his Bashaws*]
    Stand all aside, and let the knights determine,
    And send to keep our galleys under sail,   15
    For happily we shall not tarry here.—
    Now, governor, how are you resolved?

    I.ii.0.1.] The scene begins in the senate-house but later is imagined to be
at Barabas's house; see ll. 304–5.
    Governor] Q's 'Gouernors' here and at ll. 10, 17, 27, 32, and 129 suggests
that Marlowe began the play with the assumption that Malta was ruled by a
body of 'governors' and later settled the role of a single 'governor' on Ferneze
without bothering to revise his first impression.
    0.2. *Bashaws*] pashas, Turkish aristocrats and military leaders (spelled
'Bassoes' here and in l. 1 in Q but generally 'Bashaws').
    2. *Knights of Malta*] The Knights of St John of Jerusalem were stationed
on Malta beginning in 1530.
    9. *consider*] be considerate towards.
    10. *grave*] a common form of respectful address.
    11. *my father's*] i.e. Emperor of Turkey's; see l. 39. Selim succeeded his
father, Soliman the Magnificant, in 1566.
    13. *give us leave*] 'A polite request for privacy for consultation' (Bennett).
    15. *send*] send word.
    16. *happily*] with good luck, if things go well.
    17. *how . . . resolved?*] what have you decided?

Ferneze. Thus: since your hard conditions are such
    That you will needs have ten years' tribute past,
    We may have time to make collection   20
    Amongst the inhabitants of Malta for 't.
First Bashaw. That's more than is in our commission.
Calymath. What, Callapine, a little courtesy!
    Let's know their time; perhaps it is not long,
    And 'tis more kingly to obtain by peace   25
    Than to enforce conditions by constraint.—
    What respite ask you, governor?
Ferneze.   But a month.
Calymath. We grant a month, but see you keep your promise.
    Now launch our galleys back again to sea,
    Where we'll attend the respite you have ta'en,   30
    And for the money send our messenger.
    Farewell, great governor and brave knights of Malta.
Ferneze. And all good fortune wait on Calymath.
                  Exeunt [CALYMATH *and* Bashaws].
    Go one and call those Jews of Malta hither.
    Were they not summoned to appear today?   35
First Officer. They were, my lord, and here they come.

    Enter BARABAS *and three* Jews.

First Knight. Have you determined what to say to them?
Ferneze. Yes, give me leave; and Hebrews, now come near.
    From the Emperor of Turkey is arrived
    Great Selim Calymath, his highness' son,   40
    To levy of us ten years' tribute past.
    Now then, here know that it concerneth us—
Barabas. Then, good my lord, to keep your quiet still,
    Your lordship shall do well to let them have it.
Ferneze. Soft, Barabas, there's more longs to 't than so.   45

---

20. *We*] i.e. we ask that we.
22. *commission*] instructions, authority as ambassadors.
23. *Callapine*] the name, evidently, of the First Bashaw in this scene and perhaps of the Bashaw in III.v.
24. *their time*] what time they require.
30. *attend*] await.
43. *quiet*] peaceful state of affairs.
still] always, continually.
45. *there's . . . so*] there's more to it than that. (*Longs* = belongs, pertains.)

To what this ten years' tribute will amount,
That we have cast, but cannot compass it
By reason of the wars, that robbed our store;
And therefore are we to request your aid.
Barabas. Alas, my lord, we are no soldiers;   50
  And what's our aid against so great a prince?
First Knight. Tut, Jew, we know thou art no soldier;
  Thou art a merchant, and a moneyed man,
  And 'tis thy money, Barabas, we seek.
Barabas. How, my lord, my money?
Ferneze.   Thine and the rest.   55
  For, to be short, amongst you 't must be had.
First Jew. Alas, my lord, the most of us are poor!
Ferneze. Then let the rich increase your portions.
Barabas. Are strangers with your tribute to be taxed?
Second Knight.
  Have strangers leave with us to get their wealth?   60
  Then let them with us contribute.
Barabas. How, equally?
Ferneze.   No, Jew, like infidels.
  For through our sufferance of your hateful lives,
  Who stand accursèd in the sight of heaven,
  These taxes and afflictions are befall'n,   65
  And therefore thus we are determinèd:
  Read there the articles of our decrees.
Officer. (*Reads.*) 'First, the tribute-money of the Turks shall
  all be levied amongst the Jews, and each of them to pay
  one-half of his estate.'   70
Barabas. How, half his estate? [*Aside*] *I hope you mean not*
  mine.
Ferneze. Read on.

---

47. *cast*] calculated.
  compass] encompass, achieve.
  50–1.] Barabas, in pretended innocence, supposes that he and his fellow Jews are being asked to take up arms against the Turks.
  58. *increase your portions*] give extra money to bring the overall contributions to the required amount.
  59. *strangers*] aliens, foreigners.
  64.] The Jews were held responsible for the crucifixion of Christ.
  66. *are determinèd*] have resolved.

Officer. (*Reads.*) 'Secondly, he that denies to pay shall straight
    become a Christian.'
Barabas. How, a Christian? [*Aside*] H'm, what's here to do?   75
Officer. (*Reads.*) 'Lastly, he that denies this shall absolutely
    lose all he has.'
All three Jews. O, my lord, we will give half!
Barabas. O earth-mettled villains, and no Hebrews born!
    And will you basely thus submit yourselves   80
    To leave your goods to their arbitrament?
Ferneze. Why, Barabas, wilt thou be christened?
Barabas. No governor, I will be no convertite.
Ferneze. Then pay thy half.
Barabas. Why, know you what you did by this device?   85
    Half of my substance is a city's wealth.
    Governor, it was not got so easily;
    Nor will I part so slightly therewithal.
Ferneze. Sir, half is the penalty of our decree;
    Either pay that or we will seize on all.   90
Barabas. *Corpo di Dio*! Stay, you shall have half;
    Let me be used but as my brethren are.
Ferneze. No, Jew, thou hast denied the articles,
    And now it cannot be recalled.
               [*Exeunt* Officers, *on a sign from* FERNEZE.]
Barabas. Will you then steal my goods?   95
    Is theft the ground of your religion?
Ferneze. No, Jew, we take particularly thine
    To save the ruin of a multitude;
    And better one want for a common good
    Than many perish for a private man.   100

---

73. *denies*] refuses.
straight] immediately.
75. what's . . . do] what shall I do about this?
79. *earth-mettled*] having a dull or phlegmatic temperament.
81. *arbitrament*] decision, control.
88. *slightly*] easily, readily.
91. Corpo di Dio!] By God's body! (An ironic oath here, referring to the crucified Christ.)
96. *ground*] basis, fundamental principle.
99. *one want*] that one individual should go without. (Compare John, 11.50.)

> Yet, Barabas, we will not banish thee,
> But here in Malta, where thou got'st thy wealth,
> Live still; and if thou canst, get more.

Barabas. Christians, what or how can I multiply?
> Of naught is nothing made.   105

First Knight.
> From naught at first thou camest to little wealth,
> From little unto more, from more to most.
> If your first curse fall heavy on thy head,
> And make thee poor and scorned of all the world,
> 'Tis not our fault, but thy inherent sin.   110

Barabas. What? Bring you scripture to confirm your wrongs?
> Preach me not out of my possessions.
> Some Jews are wicked, as all Christians are;
> But say the tribe that I descended of
> Were all in general cast away for sin,   115
> Shall I be tried by their transgression?
> The man that dealeth righteously shall live;
> And which of you can charge me otherwise?

Ferneze. Out, wretched Barabas!
> Shamest thou not thus to justify thyself,   120
> As if we knew not thy profession?
> If thou rely upon thy righteousness,
> Be patient, and thy riches will increase.
> Excess of wealth is cause of covetousness,
> And covetousness, Oh, 'tis a monstrous sin!   125

Barabas. Ay; but theft is worse. Tush, take not from me then,
> For that is theft; and if you rob me thus,
> I must be forced to steal, and compass more.

First Knight. Grave governor, list not to his exclaims.

---

108. *your first curse*] i.e. the curse that the Jews accepted when they demanded Christ's crucifixion and said, 'His blood be on us, and on our children' (Matthew, 27.25).

115. *cast away*] rejected by God, damned.

117.] Compare Proverbs, 10.2 and 16 and 12.28, Romans, 4.13, and Galatians, 3.13–29.

119. *Out*] an expression of indignation or reproach.

121. *profession*] i.e. Old Testament religion and covetous ways.

128. *compass*] encompass; contrive an evil purpose.

129. *exclaims*] exclamations, outcries.

Convert his mansion to a nunnery;   130
His house will harbour many holy nuns.

Enter Officers.

Ferneze. It shall be so.—Now, officers, have you done?
First Officer. Ay, my lord, we have seized upon the goods
    And wares of Barabas, which being valued
    Amount to more than all the wealth in Malta,   135
    And of the other we have seizèd half;
    Then we'll take order for the residue.
Barabas. Well then, my lord, say, are you satisfied?
    You have my goods, my money, and my wealth,
    My ships, my store, and all that I enjoyed,   140
    And having all, you can request no more—
    Unless your unrelenting flinty hearts
    Suppress all pity in your stony breasts,
    And now shall move you to bereave my life.
Ferneze. No, Barabas, to stain our hands with blood   145
    Is far from us and our profession.
Barabas. Why, I esteem the injury far less
    To take the lives of miserable men
    Than be the causers of their misery.
    You have my wealth, the labour of my life,   150
    The comfort of mine age, my children's hope;
    And therefore ne'er distinguish of the wrong.
Ferneze. Content thee, Barabas, thou hast naught but right.
Barabas. Your extreme right does me exceeding wrong.
    But take it to you, i' the devil's name!   155
Ferneze. Come, let us in, and gather of these goods
    The money for this tribute of the Turk.
First Knight. 'Tis necessary that be looked unto;

---

136. *other*] other Jews.

137.] i.e. 'then we'll make arrangements for the proper disposal of all the rest'. (The line, uncertain as to exact meaning, is sometimes assigned to Ferneze.)

152. *distinguish of the wrong*] make subtle distinctions intended to minimize the wrong you have done me.

153. *right*] justice.

154. *extreme*] harsh. Accented on the first syllable.

For if we break our day, we break the league,
And that will prove but simple policy.   160
             Exeunt [FERNEZE, *Knights, and* Officers].
Barabas. Ay, policy, that's their profession,
And not simplicity as they suggest.   [*He kneels.*]
The plagues of Egypt and the curse of heaven,
Earth's barrenness, and all men's hatred,
Inflict upon them, thou great Primus Motor!   165
And here upon my knees striking the earth
I ban their souls to everlasting pains
And extreme tortures of the fiery deep
That thus have dealt with me in my distress.
First Jew. Oh, yet be patient, gentle Barabas.   170
Barabas. Oh silly brethren, born to see this day!
Why stand you thus unmoved with my laments?
Why weep you not to think upon my wrongs?
Why pine not I and die in this distress?
First Jew. Why, Barabas, as hardly can we brook   175
The cruel handling of ourselves in this.
Thou seest they have taken half our goods.
Barabas. Why did you yield to their extortion?
You were a multitude, and I but one,
And of me only have they taken all.   180
First Jew. Yet, brother Barabas, remember Job.
Barabas. What tell you me of Job? I wot his wealth
Was written thus: he had seven thousand sheep,
Three thousand camels, and two hundred yoke

---

159. *break our day*] miss our deadline.
break the league] violate our treaty obligations.
160. *simple policy*] a foolish trick.
161. *policy*] trickery, duplicity.
162. *simplicity*] honesty, lack of guile.
163. *The plagues of Egypt*] See Exodus, 7–12.
165. *Primus Motor*] First Mover.
167. *ban*] curse.
171.] i.e. 'O foolish fellow Jews, destined from birth to behold this unhappiness!'
175–6. *as . . . this*] 'we find it as difficult as you to endure our harsh treatment'.
181–208.] See Job, especially 1.3, 3.1–10, 7.3, and 7.11.
182. *I wot*] I know.

Of labouring oxen, and five hundred   185
She-asses; but for every one of those,
Had they been valued at indifferent rate,
I had at home, and in mine argosy
And other ships that came from Egypt last,
As much as would have bought his beasts and him,   190
And yet have kept enough to live upon;
So that not he, but I, may curse the day,
Thy fatal birthday, forlorn Barabas,
And henceforth wish for an eternal night,
That clouds of darkness may enclose my flesh   195
And hide these extreme sorrows from mine eyes.
For only I have toiled to inherit here
The months of vanity and loss of time,
And painful nights have been appointed me.
Second Jew. Good Barabas, be patient.
Barabas.   Ay, ay;   200
Pray leave me in my patience. You that
Were ne'er possessed of wealth are pleased with want.
But give him liberty at least to mourn
That in a field amidst his enemies
Doth see his soldiers slain, himself disarmed,   205
And knows no means of his recovery.
Ay, let me sorrow for this sudden chance;
'Tis in the trouble of my spirit I speak.
Great injuries are not so soon forgot.
First Jew. Come, let us leave him in his ireful mood.   210
Our words will but increase his ecstasy.
Second Jew. On, then. But trust me, 'tis a misery
To see a man in such affliction.
Farewell, Barabas.   *Exeunt [three* Jews].
Barabas. Ay, fare you well.   [*He rises.*] 215
See the simplicity of these base slaves,

---

187. *indifferent*] impartial.
189. *last*] most recently.
198. *vanity*] vain striving.
201. *patience*] stoical suffering (playing on *be patient*, l. 200).
202. *pleased with want*] content with having little.
206. *of*] for.
211. *ecstasy*] frenzy.

Who, for the villains have no wit themselves,
Think me to be a senseless lump of clay
That will with every water wash to dirt!
No, Barabas is born to better chance   220
And framed of finer mould than common men,
That measure naught but by the present time.
A reaching thought will search his deepest wits
And cast with cunning for the time to come,
For evils are apt to happen every day.   225

Enter ABIGAIL, *the Jew's daughter.*

But whither wends my beauteous Abigail?
Oh, what has made my lovely daughter sad?
What, woman, moan not for a little loss!
Thy father has enough in store for thee.
Abigail. Not for myself, but agèd Barabas,   230
Father, for thee lamenteth Abigail.
But I will learn to leave these fruitless tears,
And, urged thereto with my afflictions,
With fierce exclaims run to the senate-house,
And in the senate reprehend them all   235
And rend their hearts with tearing of my hair
Till they reduce the wrongs done to my father.
Barabas. No, Abigail, things past recovery
Are hardly cured with exclamations.
Be silent, daughter; sufferance breeds ease,   240
And time may yield us an occasion,
Which on the sudden cannot serve the turn.

217.] 'who, since the base wretches have no sagacity themselves'.
219.] i.e. 'that will break apart at the first shock or crisis'.
220. *chance*] fortune.
221. *framed . . . mould*] fashioned out of better quality materials.
223.] 'A person endowed with foresight will exercise his utmost ingenuity'.
224. *cast*] forecast, make arrangements in advance.
233. *with*] by.
237. *reduce*] redress, repair; diminish.
240. *sufferance*] patient endurance.
241–2.] 'and time, which cannot help us in this sudden crisis, may provide us an opportunity later on'.

Besides, my girl, think me not all so fond
As negligently to forgo so much
Without provision for thyself and me.   245
Ten thousand portagues, besides great pearls,
Rich costly jewels, and stones infinite,
Fearing the worst of this before it fell,
I closely hid.
Abigail.   Where, father?
Barabas.   In my house, my girl.
Abigail. Then shall they ne'er be seen of Barabas,   250
For they have seized upon thy house and wares.
Barabas. But they will give me leave once more, I trow,
To go into my house?
Abigail.   That may they not,
For there I left the governor placing nuns,
Displacing me; and of thy house they mean   255
To make a nunnery, where none but their own sect
Must enter in, men generally barred.
Barabas. My gold, my gold, and all my wealth is gone!
You partial heavens, have I deserved this plague?
What, will you thus oppose me, luckless stars,   260
To make me desperate in my poverty?
And knowing me impatient in distress,
Think me so mad as I will hang myself,
That I may vanish o'er the earth in air
And leave no memory that e'er I was?   265
No, I will live, nor loathe I this my life;
And since you leave me in the ocean thus
To sink or swim, and put me to my shifts,

---

243. *fond*] foolish.
246. *portagues*] Portuguese gold coins.
249. *closely*] secretly.
252. *trow*] trust.
256. *sect*] sex.
257. *generally*] completely, with no exceptions.
259. *partial*] unfair, biased.
260. *luckless*] unlucky.
263. *as*] that.
268. *put . . . shifts*] i.e. put me in a desperate position, where I must fend for myself.

I'll rouse my senses and awake myself.
Daughter, I have it! Thou perceiv'st the plight   270
Wherein these Christians have oppressèd me.
Be ruled by me, for in extremity
We ought to make bar of no policy.
Abigail. Father, whate'er it be to injure them
That have so manifestly wrongèd us,   275
What will not Abigail attempt?
Barabas.   Why, so.
Then thus: thou told'st me they have turned my house
Into a nunnery, and some nuns are there.
Abigail. I did.
Barabas.   Then, Abigail, there must my girl
Entreat the abbess to be entertained.   280
Abigail. How, as a nun?
Barabas.   Ay, daughter; for religion
Hides many mischiefs from suspicion.
Abigail. Ay, but father, they will suspect me there.
Barabas. Let 'em suspect, but be thou so precise
As they may think it done of holiness.   285
Entreat 'em fair and give them friendly speech,
And seem to them as if thy sins were great,
Till thou hast gotten to be entertained.
Abigail. Thus, father, shall I much dissemble.
Barabas.   Tush!
As good dissemble that thou never mean'st   290
As first mean truth and then dissemble it;
A counterfeit profession is better
Than unseen hypocrisy.

---

272. *ruled*] persuaded, guided.
273.] 'We mustn't scruple to use any device that will help us.'
280. *entertained*] admitted.
282. *mischiefs*] acts of wickedness, evil-doing.
284. *precise*] strict or scrupulous in religious matters.
286. *Entreat 'em fair*] deal with them courteously.
289. *shall . . . dissemble*] 'I would indeed be pretending if I behaved that way'.
290–1.] 'It is quite as good to begin with a deliberate deception as to start out honestly and then lapse into trickery.'
292–3.] i.e. 'Swearing false vows of sisterhood is better than the hypocrisy practised by most nuns, a hypocrisy so inward that it shows no visible signs.'

Abigail. Well, father, say I be entertained,
  What then shall follow?
Barabas.   This shall follow then: 295
  There have I hid, close underneath the plank
  That runs along the upper chamber floor,
  The gold and jewels which I kept for thee.
  But here they come; be cunning, Abigail.
Abigail. Then, father, go with me.
Barabas.   No, Abigail, in this   300
  It is not necessary I be seen,
  For I will seem offended with thee for 't.
  Be close, my girl, for this must fetch my gold.

Enter two friars [JACOMO *and* BERNARDINE, *an* Abbess], *and*
    [*a*] Nun. [*Barabas stands aside.*]

Jacomo. Sisters, we now
  Are almost at the new-made nunnery.   305
Abbess. The better; for we love not to be seen.
  'Tis thirty winters long since some of us
  Did stray so far amongst the multitude.
Jacomo. But, madam, this house
  And waters of this new-made nunnery   310
  Will much delight you.
Abbess. It may be so. But who comes here?
Abigail. [*Coming forward*]
  Grave abbess, and you, happy virgins' guide,
  Pity the state of a distressèd maid!
Abbess. What art thou, daughter?   315
Abigail. The hopeless daughter of a hapless Jew,

---

294. *say I be entertained*] supposing I am admitted.
296. *close*] concealed.
299. *here they come*] Barabas glances offstage, and notices the friars and nuns approaching in the distance.
301.] 'It is necessary that I not be seen.'
302. *seem*] pretend to be.
303. *close*] secretive, cunning.
310. *waters*] water-source.
313. *you . . . guide*] you friars who serve as confessors to these fortunate virgins.
316. *hopeless . . . hapless*] despairing . . . wretched (with wordplay).

The Jew of Malta, wretched Barabas,
Sometimes the owner of a goodly house,
Which they have now turned to a nunnery.

Abbess. Well, daughter, say, what is thy suit with us?   320

Abigail. Fearing the afflictions which my father feels
    Proceed from sin, or want of faith in us,
    I'd pass away my life in penitence
    And be a novice in your nunnery
    To make atonement for my labouring soul.   325

Jacomo. [*To Bernardine*]
    No doubt, brother, but this proceedeth of the spirit.

Bernardine. [*To Jacomo*]
    Ay, and of a moving spirit too, brother; but come,
    Let us entreat she may be entertained.

Abbess. Well, daughter, we admit you for a nun.

Abigail. First let me as a novice learn to frame   330
    My solitary life to your strait laws,
    And let me lodge where I was wont to lie;
    I do not doubt, by your divine precepts
    And mine own industry, but to profit much.

Barabas. (*Aside*) *As much, I hope, as all I hid is worth.*   335

Abbess. Come, daughter, follow us.

Barabas. [*Coming forward*]
    Why, how now, Abigail, what makest thou
    Amongst these hateful Christians?

Jacomo. Hinder her not, thou man of little faith,
    For she has mortified herself.

Barabas.   How, mortified?   340

Jacomo. And is admitted to the sisterhood.

---

318. *Sometimes*] formerly.

322. *in us*] in us Jews.

325. *labouring*] troubled, distressed.

326. *of the spirit*] by divine influence. Compare John, 3.5–6.

327. *moving spirit*] with wordplay suggesting sexual arousal.

330. *frame*] shape, fashion.

331. *strait*] strict, rigorous.

334–5. *industry . . . profit . . . worth*] with wordplay suggesting both spiritual and financial gain.

337. *what makest thou*] what are you doing.

340. *mortified*] become dead to the world and the flesh.

Barabas. Child of perdition and thy father's shame,
What wilt thou do among these hateful fiends?
I charge thee on my blessing that thou leave
These devils and their damnèd heresy.   345
Abigail. Father, give me—
Barabas.   Nay, back, Abigail,
And think upon the jewels and the gold;
                              (*Whispers to her.*)
The board is markèd thus that covers it.
                    [*He makes a sign of the cross.*]
Away, accursèd, from thy father's sight!
Jacomo. Barabas, although thou art in misbelief,   350
And wilt not see thine own afflictions,
Yet let thy daughter be no longer blind.
Barabas. Blind, friar? I reck not thy persuasions.
The board is markèd thus that covers it.
                    [*He makes a sign of the cross.*]
For I had rather die than see her thus.—   355
Wilt thou forsake me too in my distress,
Seducèd daughter? (*Aside to her*) *Go, forget not*—
Becomes it Jews to be so credulous?
(*Aside to her*) *Tomorrow early I'll be at the door.*
No, come not at me! If thou wilt be damned,   360
Forget me, see me not, and so be gone.
(*Aside*) *Farewell, remember tomorrow morning.*
Out, out, thou wretch!
          [*Exit* BARABAS *on one side; exeunt* ABIGAIL, Abbess,
              Friars, *and* Nun *on the other. As they go out,*]

Enter MATHIAS.

Mathias. Who's this? Fair Abigail, the rich Jew's daughter,

---

344. *charge*] command.

346. *give me*] Perhaps Abigail starts to ask her father's blessing.

350. *in misbelief*] i.e. in a state of Jewish non-belief in Christ.

352. *blind*] spiritually blind.

353. *I reck . . . persuasions*] I dismiss out of hand your creed and your arguments.

357. *Seducèd*] won away from your former faith.

358.] 'Does it do Jews credit to be so easily taken in by seductive argument?'

Become a nun? Her father's sudden fall   365
Has humbled her and brought her down to this.
Tut, she were fitter for a tale of love
Than to be tirèd out with orisons;
And better would she far become a bed,
Embracèd in a friendly lover's arms,   370
Than rise at midnight to a solemn mass.

Enter LODOWICK.

Lodowick. Why, how now, Don Mathias, in a dump?
Mathias. Believe me, noble Lodowick, I have seen
    The strangest sight, in my opinion,
    That ever I beheld.
Lodowick.   What was't, I prithee?   375
Mathias. A fair young maid scarce fourteen years of age,
    The sweetest flower in Cytherea's field,
    Cropped from the pleasures of the fruitful earth
    And strangely metamorphosed to a nun.
Lodowick. But say, what was she?
Mathias.   Why, the rich Jew's daughter.   380
Lodowick. What, Barabas, whose goods were lately seized?
    Is she so fair?
Mathias.   And matchless beautiful;
    As, had you seen her, 'twould have moved your heart—
    Though countermured with walls of brass—to love,
    Or at the least to pity.   385
Lodowick. And if she be so fair as you report,
    'Twere time well spent to go and visit her.
    How say you, shall we?
Mathias. I must and will, sir; there's no remedy.

---

368. *orisons*] prayers.
371. *solemn*] ceremonial.
372. *in a dump*] down in the dumps.
377. *Cytherea's*] Venus's.
381. *lately*] recently.
384. *countermured*] fortified with a double wall for extra defensive power.
(Q reads 'countermin'd'; compare V.iii.9.)
389.] Mathias's stiff reply suggests that the rivalry over Abigail is already established.

Lodowick. And so will I too, or it shall go hard.   390
    Farewell, Mathias.
Mathias.   Farewell, Lodowick.   *Exeunt.*

---

  390. *or . . . hard*] i.e. 'unless there be compelling reasons preventing me';
'or there will be trouble'. With suggestion of frustrated sexual arousal.

Act II

[II. i]

Enter BARABAS *with a light.*

Barabas. Thus, like the sad presaging raven that tolls
   The sick man's passport in her hollow beak,
   And in the shadow of the silent night
   Doth shake contagion from her sable wings,
   Vexed and tormented runs poor Barabas   5
   With fatal curses towards these Christians.
   The incertain pleasures of swift-footed time
   Have ta'en their flight and left me in despair;
   And of my former riches rests no more
   But bare remembrance, like a soldier's scar,   10
   That has no further comfort for his maim.
   O Thou that with a fiery pillar led'st
   The sons of Israel through the dismal shades,
   Light Abraham's offspring, and direct the hand
   Of Abigail this night! Or let the day   15
   Turn to eternal darkness after this.
   No sleep can fasten on my watchful eyes
   Nor quiet enter my distempered thoughts

II.i.1. *tolls*] sounds the funeral bell for.

2. *passport*] certificate of passage to the underworld of the dead. *Ravens* are ill omens.

4. *contagion*] Night air was thought to be noxious.
sable] black.

9. *rests*] remains.

11. *That*] who.

12. *Thou*] God, who, in a pillar of a cloud by day and a pillar of fire by night, led Moses and the Israelites out of Egypt (Exodus, 13.18–22).

14. *Light*] may you offer light and comfort to.

18. *distempered*] disordered, troubled.

Till I have answer of my Abigail.

Enter ABIGAIL *above.*

Abigail. [*To herself, as she searches*]
    Now have I happily espied a time   20
    To search the plank my father did appoint;
    And here behold, unseen, where I have found
    The gold, the pearls, and jewels which he hid.
Barabas. [*To himself*]
    Now I remember those old women's words,
    Who in my wealth would tell me winter's tales,   25
    And speak of spirits and ghosts that glide by night
    About the place where treasure hath been hid;
    And now methinks that I am one of those.
    For whilst I live, here lives my soul's sole hope,
    And when I die, here shall my spirit walk.   30
Abigail. Now that my father's fortune were so good
    As but to be about this happy place!
    'Tis not so happy; yet when we parted last,
    He said he would attend me in the morn.
    Then, gentle sleep, where'er his body rests,   35
    Give charge to Morpheus that he may dream
    A golden dream, and of the sudden walk,
    Come, and receive the treasure I have found.
Barabas. '*Bueno para todos mi ganado no era.*'
    As good go on as sit so sadly thus.   40

                          [*He sees Abigail.*]

19.1. above] in the gallery above the main stage, signifying that Abigail is appearing at a window in Barabas's house.

20. *happily*] fortunately.

21. *appoint*] point out.

25. *wealth*] days of prosperity (as contrasted with my present poverty).

36. *Morpheus*] god of dreams.

37. *of the sudden*] all of a sudden.

walk] (1) sleepwalk; (2) wake. (Q's 'walke' may be a remembrance of l. 30, but the word is intelligible as it stands.)

39.] 'My flock or wealth, good for everyone else, was of no benefit to me.' Or perhaps it should read, '*Bien para todos mi ganada no es*', 'my gain is not good for everybody'—i.e. 'I don't want to hand over the money I gained to everybody'. The Quarto has *Birn* (for *Bueno* or *Bien*) and *er* (for *era* or *es*).

But stay, what star shines yonder in the east?
The lodestar of my life, if Abigail.—
Who's there?

Abigail.   Who's that?

Barabas.   Peace, Abigail, 'tis I.

Abigail. Then, father, here receive thy happiness.

Barabas. Hast thou 't?   45

Abigail. Here—(*Throws down bags.*) Hast thou 't? There's
     more, and more, and more.

Barabas. O my girl,
     My gold, my fortune, my felicity,
     Strength to my soul, death to mine enemy:
     Welcome, the first beginner of my bliss!   50
     O Abigail, Abigail, that I had thee here too!
     Then my desires were fully satisfied.
     But I will practise thy enlargement thence.
     O girl, O gold, O beauty, O my bliss!   (*Hugs his bags.*)

Abigail. Father, it draweth towards midnight now,   55
     And 'bout this time the nuns begin to wake;
     To shun suspicion, therefore, let us part.

Barabas. Farewell, my joy, and by my fingers take
     A kiss from him that sends it from his soul.

                                        [*Exit* ABIGAIL.]

     Now, Phoebus, ope the eyelids of the day,   60
     And for the raven wake the morning lark,
     That I may hover with her in the air,
     Singing o'er these, as she does o'er her young,
     'Hermoso placer de los dineros'.   *Exit.*

41.] Compare Romeo, as he sees Juliet at her window, '*above*': 'But soft,
what light through yonder window breaks?' (*R&J*, II.ii.2).

42. *lodestar*] guiding star.

47–8.] Shakespeare seems to recall this passage when he has Shylock say:
'My daughter! O, my ducats! O, my daughter!' (*MerVen.*, II.viii.15–24,
III.i.101–5). See l. 54 below.

53. *practise*] (1) devise means for; (2) use stratagems to achieve.
enlargement] release.

56. *wake*] i.e. awaken in time for the singing of matins.

60. *Phoebus*] Apollo, god of light, identified with the sun.

61. *for*] in place of.

63. *these*] i.e. the money-bags.

64.] 'beautiful pleasure of money' (a Spanish saying).

[II. ii]

Enter FERNEZE, MARTIN DEL BOSCO, *the* Knights[, *and* Officers].

Ferneze. Now, captain, tell us whither thou art bound,
         Whence is thy ship that anchors in our road,
         And why thou cam'st ashore without our leave.
Bosco. Governor of Malta, hither am I bound;
         My ship, the *Flying Dragon*, is of Spain,   5
         And so am I: Del Bosco is my name,
         Vice-admiral unto the Catholic king.
First Knight. 'Tis true, my lord; therefore entreat him well.
Bosco. Our freight is Grecians, Turks, and Afric Moors;
         For late upon the coast of Corsica,   10
         Because we vailed not to the Turkish fleet,
         Their creeping galleys had us in the chase;
         But suddenly the wind began to rise,
         And then we luffed, and tacked, and fought at ease.
         Some have we fired, and many have we sunk,   15
         But one amongst the rest became our prize;
         The captain's slain, the rest remain our slaves,
         Of whom we would make sale in Malta here.
Ferneze. Martin del Bosco, I have heard of thee.
         Welcome to Malta and to all of us.   20
         But to admit a sale of these thy Turks
         We may not—nay, we dare not—give consent,
         By reason of a tributary league.
First Knight. Del Bosco, as thou lovest and honour'st us,

II.ii.1. *captain*] senior officer, here vice-admiral; see l. 7.

2. *road*] roadstead, harbour.

10. *late*] of late, recently.

11. *vailed not*] refused to lower our sails in a conventional gesture of respect and deference. Compare V.ii.1.

12. *creeping*] slow-moving; see n. 14 below.

14. *luffed . . . tacked*] 'momentarily spilled the wind out of our sails as we zig-zagged upwind, shifting the wind repeatedly from one bow to the other'. The *creeping* Turkish galleys could overtake Del Bosco's ships as long as a light wind gave the advantage to the galleys with their rows of oarsmen, but when the breeze stiffened the nimbler sailing vessels gained the advantage.

15. *fired*] destroyed by fire.

23. *tributary league*] treaty requiring the Maltese to pay tribute to the Turks.

Persuade our governor against the Turk;   25
This truce we have is but in hope of gold,
And with that sum he craves might we wage war.

Bosco. Will Knights of Malta be in league with Turks,
And buy it basely, too, for sums of gold?
My lord, remember that, to Europe's shame,   30
The Christian isle of Rhodes, from whence you came,
Was lately lost, and you were stated here
To be at deadly enmity with Turks.

Ferneze. Captain, we know it, but our force is small.

Bosco. What is the sum that Calymath requires?   35

Ferneze. A hundred thousand crowns.

Bosco. My lord and king hath title to this isle,
And he means quickly to expel them hence;
Therefore be ruled by me, and keep the gold.
I'll write unto his majesty for aid,   40
And not depart until I see you free.

Ferneze. On this condition shall thy Turks be sold.—
Go, officers, and set them straight in show.

                                        [*Exeunt* Officers.]

Bosco, thou shalt be Malta's general;
We and our warlike knights will follow thee   45
Against these barbarous misbelieving Turks.

Bosco. So shall you imitate those you succeed;

---

27. *he*] the Turkish Selim Calymath (and his father the emperor). The
First Knight's point is that the large tribute payment might be spent instead
on arming against the Turks with Spanish backing.

31-3.] Rhodes had been the headquarters of the Knights from the early
fourteenth century until 1522, when the Turks conquered the island after a
bitterly fought siege. In 1530 the emperor Charles V granted Malta to the
Knights (see l. 37).

32. *stated*] placed, stationed; installed in office. The Knights of Malta had
a duty, by virtue of their vows, to fight the Turks on all occasions, as l. 33
makes clear.

41. *free*] free of compulsory obligation to the Turks.

43. *set . . . show*] put the Turkish slaves on display in the market
immediately.

46. *misbelieving*] pagan.

47-51.] Del Bosco describes (inaccurately) a Turkish siege of Rhodes in
1522 when, he says, the predecessors of the Knights of Malta, at that time
still headquartered on Rhodes, were overwhelmed and wiped out. In fact,
they surrendered on terms and were permitted to leave.

For when their hideous force environed Rhodes,
Small though the number was that kept the town,
They fought it out, and not a man survived   50
To bring the hapless news to Christendom.
Ferneze. So will we fight it out. Come, let's away.
Proud-daring Calymath, instead of gold,
We'll send thee bullets wrapped in smoke and fire.
Claim tribute where thou wilt, we are resolved;   55
Honour is bought with blood, and not with gold.

Exeunt.

[II. iii]

Enter Officers *with* [ITHAMORE *and other*] Slaves.

First Officer. This is the marketplace; here let 'em stand.
Fear not their sale, for they'll be quickly bought.
Second Officer. Every one's price is written on his back,
And so much must they yield or not be sold.

Enter BARABAS.

First Officer.
Here comes the Jew; had not his goods been seized,   5
He'd give us present money for them all.
Barabas. [*Aside*] In spite of these swine-eating Christians
(Unchosen nation, never circumcised,
Such as, poor villains, were ne'er thought upon
Till Titus and Vespasian conquered us),   10
Am I become as wealthy as I was.
They hoped my daughter would ha' been a nun;

53–6.] Ferneze apostrophizes the Turkish emperor's son, who is not present.

II.iii.2. *Fear . . . sale*] don't worry that they will not all be sold.
6. *present money*] ready money, cash.
8. *Unchosen*] not chosen by God for special destiny.
9. *ne'er . . . upon*] disregarded, held in poor esteem.
10. *Titus and Vespasian*] Vespasian, the Roman commander in Palestine, suppressed the revolt of the Jews against Roman authority in 66 A.D. When he became emperor in 69, his son Titus completed the siege and capture of Jerusalem in 70 (as told in the *History of the Jewish Wars* by Flavius Josephus, first century A.D.).

But she's at home, and I have bought a house
As great and fair as is the governor's;
And there in spite of Malta will I dwell,   15
Having Ferneze's hand, whose heart I'll have—
Ay, and his son's too, or it shall go hard.
I am not of the tribe of Levi, I,
That can so soon forget an injury.
We Jews can fawn like spaniels when we please,   20
And when we grin, we bite; yet are our looks
As innocent and harmless as a lamb's.
I learned in Florence how to kiss my hand,
Heave up my shoulders when they call me dog,
And duck as low as any barefoot friar,   25
Hoping to see them starve upon a stall,
Or else be gathered for in our synagogue,
That when the offering-basin comes to me,
Even for charity I may spit into 't.
Here comes Don Lodowick, the governor's son,   30
One that I love for his good father's sake.

Enter LODOWICK.

Lodowick. [*To himself*]
I hear the wealthy Jew walked this way;
I'll seek him out, and so insinuate
That I may have a sight of Abigail,
For Don Mathias tells me she is fair.   35

16.] i.e. 'I have Ferneze's authorization to prosper, but I will settle old scores still' (playing on the proverbial connection of *heart* and *hand*).

17. *or . . . hard*] i.e. 'or know the reason why'. Only the most overpowering circumstances can prevent Barabas's revenge. See l. 95 below.

18. *tribe of Levi*] a priestly caste here imagined to be forgiving and saintly, though historical evidence hardly seems to support this characterization.

23. *Florence*] known for intrigue and for Machiavelli, a Florentine.

26. *stall*] table or bench in front of a shop for display of goods, often used at night by the homeless in Elizabethan London.

27. *be gathered for*] have a collection plate (the 'offering-basin' in l. 28) passed around for them.

29. *Even for charity*] (1) as my offering; (2) to show just how much I love them.

31. *love*] (Said ironically.)

33. *insinuate*] suavely ingratiate myself.

Barabas. [*Aside*] *Now will I show myself to have more of the*
    serpent than the dove; that is, more knave than fool.
Lodowick. Yond walks the Jew; now for fair Abigail.
Barabas. [*Aside*] *Ay, ay, no doubt but she's at your command.*
Lodowick. Barabas, thou know'st I am the governor's son.   40
Barabas. I would you were his father too, sir, that's all the
    harm I wish you. [*Aside*] *The slave looks like a hog's cheek*
    new-singed.   [*He turns away.*]
Lodowick. Whither walk'st thou, Barabas?
Barabas. No further. 'Tis a custom held with us   45
    That when we speak with Gentiles like to you
    We turn into the air to purge ourselves;
    For unto us the promise doth belong.
Lodowick. Well, Barabas, canst help me to a diamond?
Barabas. Oh, sir, your father had my diamonds.   50
    Yet I have one left that will serve your turn.
    (*Aside*) *I mean my daughter—but e'er he shall have her,*
    I'll sacrifice her on a pile of wood.
    I ha' the poison of the city for him,
    And the white leprosy.   55
Lodowick. What sparkle does it give without a foil?

39.] Barabas, aware of Lodowick's interest in Abigail, privately mocks
Lodowick's assumption that he can have her if he wishes.

41–3. *I would . . . singed*] Barabas's attempt at jocular flattery, playing on
the proverb, 'Like father, like son', seems to suggest that he can't have
enough of Lodowick and his family, though in his aside he contemptuously
compares Lodowick's pink, close-shaven cheeks to a pig singed of its bristles
(and thus especially offensive to orthodox Jews, who may not eat pork).

47. *purge*] cleanse from spiritual and physical defilement.

48. *the promise*] God's covenant given to Abraham (Genesis, 15.17–21,
17.1–22, etc.) See I.i.105 and note.

51. *serve your turn*] (The phrase often carried a sexual suggestion.)

53.] The line may recall Abraham's near-sacrifice of his son Isaac (Genesis, 22) and Agamemnon's sacrifice of his daughter Iphigenia; see I.i.137
and note.

54. poison of the city] Barabas seems to suggest that Malta, like Florence
and Ancona, is famous for its poisons. Compare II.iii.23 and III.iv.69–74.

55. white leprosy] Slimy white scales signify a fearful and unpleasant stage
of the disease.

56. *foil*] thin metallic foil placed behind or under a jewel to set off its
brilliance.

Barabas. The diamond that I talk of ne'er was foiled.
  [*Aside*] *But when he touches it, it will be foiled.—*
  Lord Lodowick, it sparkles bright and fair.
Lodowick. Is it square or pointed? Pray let me know.   60
Barabas. Pointed it is, good sir—(*Aside*) *but not for you.*
Lodowick. I like it much the better.
Barabas.   So do I too.
Lodowick. How shows it by night?
Barabas.   Outshines Cynthia's rays.
  (*Aside*) *You'll like it better far o' nights than days.*
Lodowick. And what's the price?   65
Barabas. [*Aside*] *Your life an if you have it.*—Oh, my lord,
  We will not jar about the price; come to my house, and I
  will give 't your honour—(*Aside*) *with a vengeance.*
Lodowick. No, Barabas, I will deserve it first.
Barabas. Good sir,   70
  Your father has deserved it at my hands,
  Who of mere charity and Christian ruth,
  To bring me to religious purity,
  And as it were in catechizing sort,
  To make me mindful of my mortal sins,   75
  Against my will, and whether I would or no,
  Seized all I had and thrust me out o' doors,
  And made my house a place for nuns most chaste.

57–8. *foiled . . . foiled*] provided with a foil background . . . stymied, de-
filed, dishonoured.

60. *square*] cube-shaped.

61. *Pointed*] (1) shaped to a point; (2) appointed, destined.

63. *Cynthia's*] the moon's.

64.] Barabas offers another sly sexual suggestion. (Some editors prefer to
regard this line as spoken directly to Lodowick.)

66. *an if . . . it*] if you take it, the diamond (i.e. Abigail).

67. *jar*] quarrel.

68. *give 't your honour*] (1) present Your Honour with the jewel, i.e.
Abigail; (2) give you what's coming to you.

71. *deserved it*] (1) deserved the precious jewel; (2) deserved what he'll get
from me. The double meaning continues in ll. 72–8.

72. *mere*] utter, pure.

  ruth] compassion.

74. *in catechizing sort*] as though teaching me the essentials of Christian
doctrine through a set of prescribed questions and answers.

Lodowick. No doubt your soul shall reap the fruit of it.

Barabas. Ay, but, my lord, the harvest is far off.   80
    And yet I know the prayers of those nuns
    And holy friars, having money for their pains,
    Are wondrous, *(Aside) and indeed do no man good;*
    And seeing they are not idle, but still doing,
    'Tis likely they in time may reap some fruit—   85
    I mean in fullness of perfection.

Lodowick. Good Barabas, glance not at our holy nuns.

Barabas. No, but I do it through a burning zeal,
    (Aside) Hoping ere long to set the house afire;
    For though they do awhile increase and multiply,   90
    I'll have a saying to that nunnery.—
    As for the diamond, sir, I told you of,
    Come home, and there's no price shall make us part,
    Even for your honourable father's sake.
    (Aside) It shall go hard but I will see your death.   95
    But now I must be gone to buy a slave.

Lodowick. And, Barabas, I'll bear thee company.

Barabas. Come, then; here's the marketplace.—What's the
    price of this slave? Two hundred crowns! Do the Turks
    weigh so much?   100

First Officer. Sir, that's his price.

Barabas. What, can he steal, that you demand so much?

---

82. *having . . . pains*] receiving bequests for the singing of masses. A gibe at Catholic practices of selling 'indulgences' for sins.

84. *still doing*] (1) continually doing good works; (2) incessantly sexual.

85. *reap some fruit*] (1) gain spiritual reward (as in l. 79); (2) procreate.

86. *in . . . perfection*] (1) achieving spiritual holiness; (2) coming to full term of pregnancy.

87. *glance not at*] do not offer sarcastic insinuations about.

88. *burning*] (1) fervent; (2) incendiary.

90. increase and multiply] i.e. obey God's command to Noah to populate the earth.

91. have a saying to] 'have something to say to'. Barabas ominously implies that the nuns will be hearing from him.

93. *there's . . . part*] (1) the mere matter of price will not hinder our coming to an agreement; (2) no price could induce me to let you leave my place alive.

95. It . . . but] 'unless I am prevented by overpowering circumstances'. Compare l. 17 above.

99. *crowns*] gold coins.

Belike he has some new trick for a purse;
And if he has, he is worth three hundred plates,
So that, being bought, the town seal might be got   105
To keep him for his lifetime from the gallows.
The sessions day is critical to thieves,
And few or none 'scape but by being purged.
Lodowick. Ratest thou this Moor but at two hundred plates?
First Officer. No more, my lord.   110
Barabas. Why should this Turk be dearer than that Moor?
First Officer. Because he is young and has more qualities.
Barabas. What, hast the philosopher's stone? An thou hast,
     break my head with it; I'll forgive thee.
Slave. No, sir, I can cut and shave.   115
Barabas. Let me see, sirrah; are you not an old shaver?
Slave. Alas, sir, I am a very youth.
Barabas. A youth? I'll buy you, and marry you to Lady Vanity
     if you do well.
Slave. I will serve you, sir—   120

103–6.] 'Perhaps he has some new trick for purse-snatching; if so, he is worth a lot of money, so that a slave-owner might consider him worth the purchase price if the town could be persuaded to issue a lifetime pardon protecting him from being hanged as a thief.' (Barabas is jocosely suggesting that such a rogue would be useful to his master.)

104. *plates*] Spanish silver coins.

107. *sessions day*] day on which an accused thief would be brought before the judges.

critical] crucial.

108. *purged*] (1) punished for their crimes; (2) forced to do penance.

112. *qualities*] skills, accomplishments.

113. *the philosopher's stone*] a reputed substance that was supposed to turn all materials into gold or silver. Barabas jokingly regards the slave as if he were virtually able to make money for his master.

113–14. *An . . . thee*] i.e. 'If you have this so-called philosopher's stone, and can let me have it, I wouldn't mind if you hit me over the head with it.'

115–24.] In Q, the Slave's speeches are assigned to Ithamore, but ll. 127–8 make clear that Barabas examines first one slave and then Ithamore.

116. *sirrah*] form of address to a social inferior.

shaver] (1) barber; (2) chap, fellow; (3) con artist.

118. *Lady Vanity*] The Youth of Tudor morality plays typically falls in with Vice characters like Lady Vanity.

120–1. *I will . . . other*] The Slave's 'I will be your servant' is sardonically turned by Barabas into 'You'll play a trick on me'.

Barabas. Some wicked trick or other. It may be, under colour
   of shaving, thou'lt cut my throat for my goods. Tell me,
   hast thou thy health well?
Slave. Ay, passing well.
Barabas. So much the worse. I must have one that's sickly,   125
   an't be but for sparing victuals; 'tis not a stone of beef a
   day will maintain you in these chops.—Let me see one
   that's somewhat leaner.
First Officer. [*Indicating Ithamore*]
   Here's a leaner. How like you him?
Barabas. [*To Ithamore*] Where wast thou born?   130
Ithamore. In Thrace; brought up in Arabia.
Barabas. So much the better; thou art for my turn.
   An hundred crowns? I'll have him; there's the coin.
                         [*He gives money.*]
First Officer. Then mark him, sir, and take him hence.
Barabas. [*Aside*] *Ay, mark him, you were best; for this is he*   135
   That by my help shall do much villainy.
   [*To Lodowick*] My lord, farewell.
   [*To Ithamore*]   Come, sirrah, you are mine.
   [*To Lodowick*] As for the diamond, it shall be yours.
   I pray, sir, be no stranger at my house;
   All that I have shall be at your command.   140

       Enter MATHIAS [*and* KATHERINE, *his*] *mother.*

Mathias. [*To himself*]
   What makes the Jew and Lodowick so private?
   I fear me 'tis about fair Abigail.   [*Exit* LODOWICK.]
Barabas. [*To Ithamore*]
   Yonder comes Don Mathias; let us stay.

---

121. *colour*] pretext.
124. *passing*] very.
126–7. *an 't . . . chops*] 'if only for the sake of saving the cost of feeding a
slave; even a *stone* [14 pounds] of beef daily wouldn't keep you going'.
   chops] jaws.
132. *for my turn*] suitable for my purposes.
134–5. *mark . . . mark*] brand (as a mark of ownership) . . . take good note
of, keep an eye on.
142.S.D.] The placement of Lodowick's exit, not marked in Q, is uncertain; he re-enters at l. 220.1.
143. *stay*] stay and observe.

He loves my daughter, and she holds him dear;
But I have sworn to frustrate both their hopes, 145
And be revenged upon the governor.

Katherine. [*To Mathias, as they inspect the slaves*]
This Moor is comeliest, is he not? Speak, son.

Mathias. No, this is the better, mother. View this well.

Barabas. [*Aside to Mathias*]
Seem not to know me here before your mother,
Lest she mistrust the match that is in hand. 150
When you have brought her home, come to my house;
Think of me as thy father. Son, farewell.

Mathias. But wherefore talked Don Lodowick with you?

Barabas. *Tush, man, we talked of diamonds, not of Abigail.*

Katherine. Tell me, Mathias, is not that the Jew? 155

Barabas. As for the comment on the Maccabees,
I have it, sir, and 'tis at your command.

Mathias. Yes, madam, and my talk with him was but
About the borrowing of a book or two.

Katherine. Converse not with him; he is cast off from heaven. 160
[*To Officer*] Thou hast thy crowns, fellow.
[*To Mathias*]   Come, let's away.

Mathias. [*To Barabas*] Sirrah Jew, remember the book.

Barabas. Marry will I, sir.

                    Exeunt [MATHIAS, KATHERINE, *and* Slave].

First Officer. Come, I have made a reasonable market; let's
    away.   [*Exeunt* Officers *with* Slaves.] 165

144–6.] These lines could be spoken aside, but Barabas has already indi-
cated at ll. 135–6 that he will use Ithamore to carry out his villainy. Some
editors see ll. 143–6 as addressed to Lodowick, before he exits; see 142.S.D.,
note.

146.] Q's use of a dash in 'upon the—Governor' leaves open the possibil-
ity that Barabas says this last word aside, having addressed the previous
speech to Lodowick or Ithamore; see previous note.

150. mistrust] suspect.

153. wherefore] why.

156–7.] Barabas speaks aloud in such a way as to explain his whispering
with Mathias, in order to allay Katherine's suspicions. He pretends that he is
offering to loan Mathias a commentary on the two Apocryphal books of the
Bible that depict the deliverance of Judea from Syrian persecution in 175–164
B.C. Compare note at II.iii.10 above.

163.1.] This stage direction assumes that Katherine and Mathias have
purchased a slave.

Barabas. Now, let me know thy name, and therewithal
    Thy birth, condition, and profession.
Ithamore. Faith, sir, my birth is but mean, my name's
    Ithamore, my profession what you please.
Barabas. Hast thou no trade? Then listen to my words,   170
    And I will teach thee that shall stick by thee.
    First, be thou void of these affections:
    Compassion, love, vain hope, and heartless fear.
    Be moved at nothing; see thou pity none,
    But to thyself smile when the Christians moan.   175
Ithamore. Oh, brave, master, I worship your nose for this!
Barabas. As for myself, I walk abroad o' nights,
    And kill sick people groaning under walls;
    Sometimes I go about and poison wells;
    And now and then, to cherish Christian thieves,   180
    I am content to lose some of my crowns,
    That I may, walking in my gallery,
    See 'em go pinioned along by my door.
    Being young, I studied physic, and began
    To practise first upon the Italian;   185
    There I enriched the priests with burials,

---

167. *condition*] social status, position.

168. *mean*] of low social position.

169. *Ithamore*] probably a version of Ithamar, one of Aaron's sons, first mentioned in Exodus, 6.23.

171. *that . . . thee*] that which will be worth your remembering and will stand you in good stead.

172. *affections*] feelings, emotions.

173. *heartless*] cowardly.

176. *brave*] splendid! wonderful!

nose] The epithet here suggests that the actor playing Barabas wore a large false nose; see III.iii.10 and IV.i.25. On the other hand, James Shapiro, in *Shakespeare and the Jews* (1995), warns against too easy assumptions of such visual labelling of Jewish figures on the Elizabethan stage.

180–3.] Presumably, Barabas uses some of his money as a trap for thieves, so that they will be apprehended and executed.

182. *gallery*] balcony.

183. *pinioned*] with arms tied together or shackled.

184. *Being young*] when I was a young man.

physic] medicine.

185. *the Italian*] Italians.

And always kept the sexton's arms in ure
With digging graves and ringing dead men's knells;
And after that was I an engineer,
And in the wars 'twixt France and Germany,   190
Under pretence of helping Charles the Fifth,
Slew friend and enemy with my stratagems.
Then after that was I an usurer,
And with extorting, cozening, forfeiting,
And tricks belonging unto brokery,   195
I filled the jails with bankrupts in a year,
And with young orphans planted hospitals,
And every moon made some or other mad,
And now and then one hang himself for grief,
Pinning upon his breast a long great scroll   200
How I with interest tormented him.
But mark how I am blest for plaguing them:
I have as much coin as will buy the town!
But tell me now, how hast thou spent thy time?
Ithamore. Faith, master,   205
In setting Christian villages on fire,
Chaining of eunuchs, binding galley-slaves.
One time I was an ostler in an inn,
And in the night-time secretly would I steal
To travellers' chambers and there cut their throats.   210
Once at Jerusalem, where the pilgrims kneeled,
I strowèd powder on the marble stones,

---

187. *ure*] use, practice.
189. *engineer*] constructor of military works and devices.
191. *Charles the Fifth*] Habsburg emperor of Spain and Germany.
194. *cozening*] cheating.
forfeiting] subjecting a borrower to forfeiture or confiscation because of that person's inability to repay.
195. *brokery*] trafficking as a broker.
197.] 'and filled the orphanages'.
198. *moon*] month. (The moon was widely supposed to influence the insane.)
199. *one hang*] caused someone to hang.
201. *with interest*] with threats of foreclosure for interest payment due.
208. *ostler*] The stable-men who tended to travellers' horses were notoriously dishonest.

And therewithal their knees would rankle, so
That I have laughed a-good to see the cripples
Go limping home to Christendom on stilts.   215
Barabas. Why, this is something! Make account of me
  As of thy fellow; we are villains both;
  Both circumcisèd, we hate Christians both.
  Be true and secret, thou shalt want no gold.
  But stand aside; here comes Don Lodowick.   220

Enter LODOWICK.

Lodowick. Oh, Barabas, well met.
  Where is the diamond you told me of?
Barabas. I have it for you, sir; please you walk in with me.—
  What ho, Abigail! Open the door, I say.

Enter ABIGAIL [*with letters*].

Abigail. In good time, father. Here are letters come   225
  From Ormuz, and the post stays here within.
Barabas. Give me the letters. Daughter, do you hear?
  Entertain Lodowick, the governor's son,
  With all the courtesy you can afford,
  Provided that you keep your maidenhead.   230
  Use him as if he were a—*Philistine.   Aside* [*to Abigail*].
  Dissemble, swear, protest, vow to love him;
  He is not of the seed of Abraham.—
  I am a little busy, sir, pray pardon me.—
  Abigail, bid him welcome for my sake.   235

---

213. *rankle*] fester.
214. *a-good*] heartily.
215. *stilts*] crutches.
216–17. *Make . . . fellow*] consider yourself my friend.
223. *walk in*] The scene, which began at the slave market, is now imagined
to be in front of Barabas's house—possibly nearby.
225. *In good time*] You arrive at the right time.
226. *Ormuz*] a trading city at the mouth of the Persian Gulf.
post] messenger.
227–31.] Some of this speech could be aside to Abigail, but as marked in
Q and in this edition the speech may well be Barabas's sexist joking intended
to raise Lodowick's hopes.
231. Philistine] a Palestinian tribe on unfriendly terms with the Jews.
232. protest] make protestations of affection.

Abigail. For your sake and his own he's welcome hither.
Barabas. Daughter, a word more. *Kiss him, speak him fair,*
                                        [*Aside to Abigail*]
    And like a cunning Jew so cast about
    That ye be both made sure ere you come out.
Abigail. Oh, father, Don Mathias is my love!   240
Barabas. I know it; yet I say make love to him.
    Do; it is requisite it should be so.—
    Nay, on my life it is my factor's hand.
    But go you in; I'll think upon the account.
                          [*Exeunt* LODOWICK *and* ABIGAIL.]
    The account is made, for Lodowick dies.   245
    My factor sends me word a merchant's fled
    That owes me for a hundred tun of wine.
    I weigh it thus much; I have wealth enough.
    For now by this has he kissed Abigail,
    And she vows love to him, and he to her.   250
    As sure as heaven rained manna for the Jews,
    So sure shall he and Don Mathias die.
    His father was my chiefest enemy.

Enter MATHIAS.

    Whither goes Don Mathias? Stay a while.
Mathias. Whither but to my fair love Abigail?   255
Barabas. Thou know'st, and heaven can witness it is true,
    That I intend my daughter shall be thine.
Mathias. Ay, Barabas, or else thou wrong'st me much.
Barabas. Oh, heaven forbid I should have such a thought!

---

237. speak him fair] talk to him courteously.
238. cast about] manage the business.
239. made sure] betrothed.
241. him] Lodowick.
243. *factor's hand*] agent's handwriting. Barabas pretends that he and
Abigail have been discussing the letter she gave him.
244–5. *the account . . . The account*] the agent's handling of my
account . . . Lodowick's fate.
248. *thus much*] i.e. worth a snap of the fingers.
249. *by this*] by this time.
251. *manna*] a dewlike food from heaven that sustained the Israelites
during their wandering in the wilderness (Exodus, 16.13–15 and 35, Numbers, 11.6ff., Joshua, 5.12).

Pardon me though I weep; the governor's son   260
Will, whether I will or no, have Abigail.
He sends her letters, bracelets, jewels, rings.
Mathias. Does she receive them?
Barabas. She? No, Mathias, no, but sends them back,
And when he comes, she locks herself up fast;   265
Yet through the keyhole will he talk to her,
While she runs to the window, looking out
When you should come and hale him from the door.
Mathias. Oh, treacherous Lodowick!
Barabas. Even now as I came home, he slipped me in,   270
And I am sure he is with Abigail.
Mathias. I'll rouse him thence.   [*He draws his sword.*]
Barabas. Not for all Malta! Therefore sheath your sword.
If you love me, no quarrels in my house,
But steal you in and seem to see him not;   275
I'll give him such a warning ere he goes
As he shall have small hopes of Abigail.
Away, for here they come.

Enter LODOWICK [*and*] ABIGAIL.

Mathias. What, hand in hand? I cannot suffer this.
Barabas. Mathias, as thou lovest me, not a word.   280
Mathias. Well, let it pass. Another time shall serve.   *Exit.*
Lodowick. Barabas, is not that the widow's son?
Barabas. Ay, and take heed, for he hath sworn your death.
Lodowick. My death? What, is the base-born peasant mad?
Barabas. No, no; but happily he stands in fear   285
Of that which you, I think, ne'er dream upon,

---

265. *fast*] securely.
268. *When . . . come*] to see if you have come.
hale] pull violently, drag.
270. *slipped me in*] slipped in past me.
272. *rouse*] force out of hiding, as though he were hunted game.
277. *As*] that.
279. *suffer*] endure, allow.
285. *happily*] perhaps.
285–6. *stands . . . upon*] 'is fearful of losing Abigail to you, my lord, even though we know of course that you have no such intention'. (The latter part of this statement is said ironically, perhaps to arouse Lodowick's competitive instincts.)

My daughter here, a paltry silly girl.
Lodowick. Why, loves she Don Mathias?
Barabas. Does she not with her smiling answer you?
Abigail. [*Aside*] *He has my heart; I smile against my will.*   290
Lodowick.
    Barabas, thou know'st I have loved thy daughter long.
Barabas. And so has she done you, even from a child.
Lodowick. And now I can no longer hold my mind.
Barabas. Nor I the affection that I bear to you.
Lodowick. This is thy diamond. Tell me, shall I have it?   295
Barabas. Win it and wear it; it is yet unsoiled.
    Oh, but I know your lordship would disdain
    To marry with the daughter of a Jew;
    And yet I'll give her many a golden cross,
    With Christian posies round about the ring.   300
Lodowick. 'Tis not thy wealth, but her, that I esteem;
    Yet crave I thy consent.
Barabas. And mine you have; yet let me talk to her.
    This offspring of Cain, this Jebusite,   *Aside* [*to Abigail*]
    That never tasted of the Passover,   305
    Nor e'er shall see the land of Canaan,
    Nor our Messias that is yet to come,
    This gentle maggot, Lodowick, I mean,

---

287. *silly*] simple, unsophisticated.

290. He] Mathias.

293. *hold my mind*] hold back from saying what I feel.

296. *unsoiled*] unsullied, not dirtied. Perhaps it should read *unfoiled*: (1) unprovided with a background to set it off; (2) unsullied. (Q reads 'vnsoyl'd'.)

299. *cross*] coin stamped with a cross.

300. *posies*] mottoes.

304. offspring of Cain] descendant of the first murderer on earth (Genesis, 4).

Jebusite] Canaanite inhabitant of Jerusalem before its capture by King David (2 Samuel, 5.6–10), not a worshipper of the true God.

306. land of Canaan] promised to the Israelites as part of God's covenant (Genesis, 17.8).

307. Messias] The Israelites refused to believe that Christ was truly the Messiah fulfilling Old Testament prophecy.

308. gentle] (1) of good birth; (2) a maggot (the larva of the bluebottle); (3) a gentile, non-Jew.

    Must be deluded. Let him have thy hand,
      But keep thy heart till Don Mathias comes.   310
Abigail. What, shall I be betrothed to Lodowick?
Barabas. It's no sin to deceive a Christian,
    For they themselves hold it a principle
    Faith is not to be held with heretics;
    But all are heretics that are not Jews.   315
    This follows well, and therefore, daughter, fear not.—
    I have entreated her, and she will grant.
Lodowick. Then, gentle Abigail, plight thy faith to me.
Abigail. [*Aside*] *I cannot choose, seeing my father bids.—*
    Nothing but death shall part my love and me.   320
Lodowick. Now have I that for which my soul hath longed.
Barabas. (*Aside*) *So have not I, but yet I hope I shall.*
Abigail. [*Aside*] *O wretched Abigail, what hast thou done?*
Lodowick. Why on the sudden is your colour changed?
Abigail. I know not, but farewell; I must be gone.   325
Barabas. [*Aside to Ithamore*]
    Stay her, but let her not speak one word more.
                [*Ithamore restrains Abigail.*]
Lodowick. Mute o' the sudden? Here's a sudden change.
Barabas. Oh, muse not at it; 'tis the Hebrews' guise
    That maidens new-betrothed should weep a while.
    Trouble her not; sweet Lodowick, depart.   330
    She is thy wife, and thou shalt be mine heir.
Lodowick. Oh, is 't the custom? Then I am resolved;
    But rather let the brightsome heavens be dim,
    And nature's beauty choke with stifling clouds,
    Than my fair Abigail should frown on me.   335

               Enter MATHIAS.

There comes the villain. Now I'll be revenged.

314–15.] i.e. 'Christians flatly claim that they need not keep promises made to heretics; by the same logic, for us Jews all non-Jews are heretics and need not be treated honourably.'

318. *plight thy faith*] give your promise of betrothal.

319.] Although plausibly an aside, this speech might instead have been spoken aloud, in a tone of coy reluctance designed to encourage Lodowick.

320. *my love and me*] (1) my promise of love to you; (2) Mathias and me.

328. *guise*] custom.

332. *resolved*] satisfied, answered.

Barabas. Be quiet, Lodowick. It is enough
   That I have made thee sure to Abigail.
Lodowick. Well, let him go.   *Exit.*
Barabas. [*To Mathias*]
   Well, but for me, as you went in at doors   340
   You had been stabbed; but not a word on 't now.
   Here must no speeches pass, nor swords be drawn.
Mathias. Suffer me, Barabas, but to follow him.
Barabas. No. So shall I, if any hurt be done,
   Be made an accessory of your deeds.   345
   Revenge it on him when you meet him next.
Mathias. For this I'll have his heart.
Barabas. Do so. Lo, here I give thee Abigail.
Mathias. What greater gift can poor Mathias have?
   Shall Lodowick rob me of so fair a love?   350
   My life is not so dear as Abigail.
Barabas. My heart misgives me that, to cross your love,
   He's with your mother; therefore after him.
Mathias. What, is he gone unto my mother?
Barabas. Nay, if you will, stay till she comes herself.   355
Mathias. I cannot stay; for if my mother come
   She'll die with grief.   *Exit.*
Abigail. I cannot take my leave of him for tears.
   Father, why have you thus incensed them both?
Barabas. What's that to thee?
Abigail.   I'll make 'em friends again.   360
Barabas. You'll make 'em friends?
   Are there not Jews enough in Malta
   But thou must dote upon a Christian?
Abigail. I will have Don Mathias; he is my love.
Barabas. Yes, you shall have him. [*To Ithamore*] Go put her
   in.   365

---

   343. *Suffer*] allow. Evidently Barabas restrains Mathias in the next line in order to prolong the scene and then goads him into action at l. 353.

   352. *misgives me*] makes me fear.

   cross] thwart, hinder.

   355.] i.e. 'If you don't believe me, wait and see when your mother comes—when it will be too late.'

   357. *grief*] i.e. grief at having her son marry a Jewess.

   358.] 'I could not even say goodbye to Mathias, I was weeping so.'

   365. *put her in*] force her into the house.

Ithamore. Ay, I'll put her in.   [*He puts* ABIGAIL *in.*]

Barabas. Now tell me, Ithamore, how likest thou this?

Ithamore. Faith, master, I think by this you purchase both
   their lives; is it not so?

Barabas. True; and it shall be cunningly performed.   370

Ithamore. Oh, master, that I might have a hand in this!

Barabas. Ay, so thou shalt; 'tis thou must do the deed.
   Take this and bear it to Mathias straight,
                                      [*He gives him a letter.*]
   And tell him that it comes from Lodowick.

Ithamore. 'Tis poisoned, is it not?   375

Barabas. No, no; and yet it might be done that way.
   It is a challenge feigned from Lodowick.

Ithamore. Fear not; I'll so set his heart afire that he shall verily
   think it comes from him.

Barabas. I cannot choose but like thy readiness;   380
   Yet be not rash, but do it cunningly.

Ithamore. As I behave myself in this, employ me hereafter.

Barabas. Away, then.   *Exit* [ITHAMORE].
   So. Now will I go in to Lodowick,
   And like a cunning spirit feign some lie   385
   Till I have set 'em both at enmity.   *Exit.*

368–9. *purchase . . . lives*] plot their deaths.
375. *poisoned*] i.e. with poisoned perfume.

Act III

Enter [BELLAMIRA] *a Courtesan.*

Bellamira. Since this town was besieged, my gain grows cold.
    The time has been that but for one bare night
    A hundred ducats have been freely given;
    But now against my will I must be chaste,
    And yet I know my beauty doth not fail.   5
    From Venice merchants, and from Padua
    Were wont to come rare-witted gentlemen,
    Scholars, I mean, learnèd and liberal;
    And now, save Pilia-Borza, comes there none,
    And he is very seldom from my house;   10
    And here he comes.

Enter PILIA-BORZA.

Pilia-Borza. Hold thee, wench. There's something for thee to
    spend.   *[He gives her money from a bag.]*
Bellamira. 'Tis silver. I disdain it.
Pilia-Borza. Ay, but the Jew has gold,   15
    And I will have it, or it shall go hard.
Bellamira. Tell me, how camest thou by this?

III.i.1. *Since*] ever since.
my gain . . . cold] i.e. business is terrible.
2. *bare*] (1) single; (2) naked.
3. *ducats*] gold coins.
7. *rare-witted*] very witty, cultivated.
8. *liberal*] (1) well educated; (2) free-spending.
9. *Pilia-Borza*] literally, 'take-purse' (from the Italian *pigliare*).
10. *from*] absent from.
12. *Hold thee*] here, take this.
16. *or . . . hard*] unless I encounter insuperable difficulties (with a suggestion, as at I.ii.390, of male sexual arousal).

Pilia-Borza. Faith, walking the back lanes through the gar-
dens I chanced to cast mine eye up to the Jew's counting-
house, where I saw some bags of money, and in the night   20
I clambered up with my hooks, and as I was taking my
choice I heard a rumbling in the house; so I took only this
and run my way. But here's the Jew's man.

Enter ITHAMORE.

Bellamira. Hide the bag.
Pilia-Borza. Look not towards him; let's away. Zounds, what   25
a looking thou keep'st! Thou'lt betray 's anon.
[*Exeunt* BELLAMIRA *and* PILIA-BORZA.]
Ithamore. Oh, the sweetest face that ever I beheld! I know she
is a courtesan by her attire. Now would I give a hundred
of the Jew's crowns that I had such a concubine.
Well, I have delivered the challenge in such sort   30
As meet they will, and fighting die. Brave sport!
Exit.

[III. ii]

Enter MATHIAS.

Mathias. This is the place. Now Abigail shall see
Whether Mathias holds her dear or no.

Enter LODOWICK *reading.*

---

18. *Faith*] in faith.
21. *hooks*] climbing hooks, used by professional thieves.
25-6. *Zounds . . . anon*] 'By God's wounds, what a tell-tale guilty look you
throw at him! You'll give away our secret before you know it.'
31. *As . . . will*] that Lodowick and Mathias are sure to meet. (For the
challenge, see II.iii.377.)
Brave] (1) excellent; (2) courageous.

III.ii.2.1. reading] Lodowick appears to be reading Mathias's reply to
the feigned challenge that Ithamore delivered to Mathias as though it had
been written by Lodowick (see II.iii.373–86), but the assignment of l. 3 to
Mathias and l. 4 to Lodowick in Q makes the sequence of letters a little
uncertain.

Lodowick. What, dares the villain write in such base terms?
Mathias. I did it, and revenge it if thou darest.

[*They*] *fight.*

Enter BARABAS *above.*

Barabas. Oh, bravely fought! And yet they thrust not home.   5
    Now, Lodowick; now, Mathias; so!   [*Both fall dead.*]
    So; now they have showed themselves to be tall fellows.
[*Voices*] *within.* Part 'em, part 'em!
Barabas. Ay, part 'em now they are dead. Farewell, farewell.

Exit [*above*].

Enter FERNEZE, KATHERINE [, *and* Citizens *of Malta*].

Ferneze. What sight is this? My Lodowick slain!   10
    These arms of mine shall be thy sepulchre.
Katherine. Who is this? My son Mathias slain!
Ferneze. O Lodowick, hadst thou perished by the Turk,
    Wretched Ferneze might have venged thy death.
Katherine. Thy son slew mine, and I'll revenge his death.   15
Ferneze. Look, Katherine, look, thy son gave mine these
    wounds.
Katherine. Oh, leave to grieve me! I am grieved enough.
Ferneze. Oh, that my sighs could turn to lively breath,
    And these my tears to blood, that he might live!
Katherine. Who made them enemies?   20
Ferneze. I know not, and that grieves me most of all.
Katherine. My son loved thine.
Ferneze.   And so did Lodowick him.

3.] Lodowick, not knowing that Mathias has received a letter purportedly written by Lodowick, bridles at Mathias's angry manner of writing.

4.] Mathias acknowledges writing the letter that Lodowick is carrying, without realizing that Lodowick did not write the original insulting letter.

5. *home*] deeply, to the heart.

7. *tall*] brave.

8.S.D. within] offstage, as from the town.

13–14.] Ferneze, as a gentleman, cannot avenge his son's death on the woman whom he holds responsible. In l. 15, Katherine acknowledges no such constraint on her part.

17. *leave*] cease.

18. *lively*] necessary to life, vital.

Katherine. Lend me that weapon that did kill my son,
    And it shall murder me.
Ferneze. Nay, madam, stay; that weapon was my son's,   25
    And on that rather should Ferneze die.
Katherine. Hold; let's enquire the causers of their deaths,
    That we may venge their blood upon their heads.
Ferneze. Then take them up, and let them be interred
    Within one sacred monument of stone,   30
    Upon which altar I will offer up
    My daily sacrifice of sighs and tears,
    And with my prayers pierce impartial heavens,
    Till they reveal the causers of our smarts,
    Which forced their hands divide united hearts.   35
    Come, Katherine, our losses equal are.
    Then of true grief let us take equal share.

                     Exeunt [with the bodies].

[III. iii]

               Enter ITHAMORE.

Ithamore. Why, was there ever seen such villainy,
    So neatly plotted and so well performed?
    Both held in hand, and flatly both beguiled?

               Enter ABIGAIL.

Abigail. Why, how now, Ithamore, why laugh'st thou so?
Ithamore. Oh, mistress, ha, ha, ha!   5
Abigail. Why, what ail'st thou?
Ithamore. Oh, my master!
Abigail. Ha!
Ithamore. Oh, mistress, I have the bravest, gravest, secret,

---

28. *their blood . . . heads*] our sons' blood upon the murderers' heads.
33. *impartial*] i.e. unmoved, unheeding; or, partial.
34. *reveal*] Not in Q. The missing word might also possibly be 'disclose'.
smarts] pains, sorrows.
35. *divide*] to divide.

III.iii.3. *Both . . . hand*] both Lodowick and Mathias were led on.
flatly] decisively, completely.
9. *bravest*] best, finest.

subtle, bottle-nosed knave to my master that ever gentle-   10
man had.

Abigail. Say, knave, why rail'st upon my father thus?

Ithamore. Oh, my master has the bravest policy.

Abigail. Wherein?

Ithamore. Why, know you not?   15

Abigail. Why, no.

Ithamore. Know you not of Mathias' and Don Lodowick's
disaster?

Abigail. No, what was it?

Ithamore. Why, the devil invented a challenge, my master writ   20
it, and I carried it, first to Lodowick and imprimis to
Mathias.

And then they met, and as the story says,

In doleful wise they ended both their days.

Abigail. And was my father furtherer of their deaths?   25

Ithamore. Am I Ithamore?

Abigail. Yes.

Ithamore. So sure did your father write and I carry the
challenge.

Abigail. Well, Ithamore, let me request thee this: 30

Go to the new-made nunnery, and enquire

For any of the friars of Saint Jacques,

And say, I pray them come and speak with me.

Ithamore. I pray, mistress, will you answer me to one
question?   35

Abigail. Well, sirrah, what is 't?

---

10. *bottle-nosed*] with a bottle-shaped, swollen nose. Compare II.iii.176
and note.

to] as.

12. *why rail'st upon*] why do you mockingly abuse.

13. *policy*] cunning device.

21. *imprimis*] 'in the first place'. Perhaps Ithamore tries to say, with comic
ineptness, that he carried a letter to Lodowick and before that a letter to
Mathias. See II.iii.373–86 and III.ii.2.1, note.

24.] Ithamore sardonically reverses the usual ending of 'They lived happily ever after'.

32. *friars . . . Jacques*] black friars, or Dominicans, so called because in
1218 they were given the hospital of St Jacques in Paris, which became the
headquarters of their order.

33. *them*] i.e. any of them.

Ithamore. A very feeling one: have not the nuns fine sport with
    the friars now and then?

Abigail. Go to, sirrah sauce, is this your question? Get ye
    gone.   40

Ithamore. I will, forsooth, mistress.   *Exit.*

Abigail. Hard-hearted father, unkind Barabas,
    Was this the pursuit of thy policy,
    To make me show them favour severally,
    That by my favour they should both be slain?   45
    Admit thou lovedst not Lodowick for his sire,
    Yet Don Mathias ne'er offended thee.
    But thou wert set upon extreme revenge,
    Because the prior dispossessed thee once,
    And couldst not venge it but upon his son,   50
    Nor on his son but by Mathias' means,
    Nor on Mathias but by murdering me.
    But I perceive there is no love on earth,
    Pity in Jews, nor piety in Turks.
    But here comes cursèd Ithamore with the friar.   55

Enter ITHAMORE [*and*] *Friar* [JACOMO].

Jacomo. Virgo, salve!

Ithamore. When, duck you?

Abigail. Welcome, grave friar. Ithamore, be gone.
                              Exit [ITHAMORE].
    Know, holy sir, I am bold to solicit thee.

Jacomo. Wherein?   60

Abigail. To get me be admitted for a nun.

---

37. *feeling*] (1) deeply felt; (2) erotic.

39. *sirrah sauce*] impudent fellow.

42. *unkind*] (1) harsh; (2) unnatural, devoid of family feeling.

43. *pursuit*] purpose, intention. (Accented on the first syllable.)

44. *severally*] separately, individually.

45. *by my favour*] through their love for me. (Playing on *favour* in l. 44.)

46. *Admit*] granted that, even if we admit.

49. *prior*] i.e. Ferneze, commander of the Maltese Knights. (Often emended to *sire*.)

56. Virgo, salve!] i.e. Hail, maiden! (With blasphemous recollection of the *Ave Maria* or Hail Mary, Luke, 1.28.)

57. *When*] an exclamation of impatience and scorn directed here at the friars' habit of genuflecting and curtsying.

Jacomo. Why, Abigail, it is not yet long since
    That I did labour thy admission,
    And then thou didst not like that holy life.
Abigail. Then were my thoughts so frail and unconfirmed,   65
    And I was chained to follies of the world;
    But now experience, purchasèd with grief,
    Has made me see the difference of things.
    My sinful soul, alas, hath paced too long
    The fatal labyrinth of misbelief,   70
    Far from the Son that gives eternal life.
Jacomo. Who taught thee this?
Abigail.   The abbess of the house,
    Whose zealous admonition I embrace.
    Oh, therefore, Jacomo, let me be one,
    Although unworthy, of that sisterhood.   75
Jacomo. Abigail, I will, but see thou change no more,
    For that will be most heavy to thy soul.
Abigail. That was my father's fault.
Jacomo.   Thy father's? How?
Abigail. Nay, you shall pardon me. *[Aside] Oh, Barabas,*
    Though thou deservest hardly at my hands,   80
    Yet never shall these lips bewray thy life.
Jacomo. Come, shall we go?
Abigail.   My duty waits on you.   *Exeunt.*

[III. iv]

Enter BARABAS *reading a letter.*

Barabas. What, Abigail become a nun again?
    False and unkind! What, hast thou lost thy father,
    And, all unknown and unconstrained of me,
    Art thou again got to the nunnery?

---

63. *labour*] work hard for, urge strenuously.
71. *Son*] Christ; with a suggestion also of *sun.*
73. *admonition*] admonishing, censure.
79. *pardon me*] excuse my not answering that.
80. *hardly*] to be treated severely.
81. *bewray*] expose to danger by revealing secrets.
82. *My duty . . . you*] I dutifully attend you and follow.

Now here she writes, and wills me to repent.　　　　5
Repentance? *Spurca*! What pretendeth this?
I fear she knows ('tis so) of my device
In Don Mathias' and Lodovico's deaths.
If so, 'tis time that it be seen into,
For she that varies from me in belief　　　　10
Gives great presumption that she loves me not,
Or, loving, doth dislike of something done.

[*Enter* ITHAMORE.]

But who comes here? O Ithamore, come near;
Come near, my love, come near, thy master's life,
My trusty servant, nay, my second self!　　　　15
For I have now no hope but even in thee,
And on that hope my happiness is built.
When saw'st thou Abigail?
Ithamore. Today.
Barabas. With whom?　　　　20
Ithamore. A friar.
Barabas. A friar? False villain, he hath done the deed.
Ithamore. How, sir?
Barabas. Why, made mine Abigail a nun.
Ithamore. That's no lie, for she sent me for him.　　　　25
Barabas. Oh, unhappy day!
False, credulous, inconstant Abigail!
But let 'em go, and, Ithamore, from hence
Ne'er shall she grieve me more with her disgrace;
Ne'er shall she live to inherit aught of mine,　　　　30
Be blessed of me, nor come within my gates,
But perish underneath my bitter curse,
Like Cain by Adam for his brother's death.

III.iv.5. *wills*] wishes, urges.
　6. Spurca] from Italian, *sporco*, 'dirty, filthy'; as it is in the feminine form, it may be directed at Abigail herself.
　pretendeth] portends.
　9. *seen into*] looked into, dealt with.
　15. *self*] Q's 'life' can be defended, but may well be a repetition of the last word in the previous line.
　33.] In Genesis, 4.9–16, God curses Cain for murdering his brother Abel.

Ithamore. Oh, master!

Barabas. Ithamore, entreat not for her. I am moved,   35
    And she is hateful to my soul and me;
    And, 'less thou yield to this that I entreat,
    I cannot think but that thou hat'st my life.

Ithamore. Who, I, master? Why, I'll run to some rock and
    throw myself headlong into the sea. Why, I'll do anything   40
    for your sweet sake.

Barabas. O trusty Ithamore, no servant, but my friend!
    I here adopt thee for mine only heir.
    All that I have is thine when I am dead,
    And whilst I live use half; spend as myself.   45
    Here, take my keys—I'll give 'em thee anon.
    Go buy thee garments—but thou shalt not want;
    Only know this, that thus thou art to do.
    But first go fetch me in the pot of rice
    That for our supper stands upon the fire.   50

Ithamore. [*Aside*] *I hold my head my master's hungry.*—I go,
    sir.   *Exit.*

Barabas. Thus every villain ambles after wealth,
    Although he ne'er be richer than in hope.
    But husht.   55

        Enter ITHAMORE *with the pot.*

Ithamore. Here 'tis, master.

Barabas. Well said, Ithamore.
    What, hast thou brought the ladle with thee too?

Ithamore. Yes, sir. The proverb says, he that eats with the
    devil had need of a long spoon. I have brought you a   60
    ladle.

Barabas. Very well, Ithamore, then now be secret.
    And for thy sake, whom I so dearly love,

---

35. *moved*] angry.

46-7.] Barabas seems to promise and then postpone the actual giving of money for garments.

48. *thus . . . do*] this is what you can expect.

51. *hold*] bet.

55. *husht*] hush.

57. *Well said*] well done.

Now shalt thou see the death of Abigail,
That thou mayst freely live to be my heir.   65
Ithamore. Why, master, will you poison her with a mess of
   rice-porridge, that will preserve life, make her round and
   plump, and batten more than you are aware?
Barabas. Ay, but Ithamore, seest thou this?
                              [*He brings out poison.*]
   It is a precious powder that I bought   70
   Of an Italian in Ancona once,
   Whose operation is to bind, infect,
   And poison deeply, yet not appear
   In forty hours after it is ta'en.
Ithamore. How, master?   75
Barabas. Thus, Ithamore:
   This even, they use in Malta here ('tis called
   Saint Jacques' Even), and then I say they use
   To send their alms unto the nunneries.
   Among the rest bear this, and set it there.   80
   There's a dark entry where they take it in,
   Where they must neither see the messenger
   Nor make enquiry who hath sent it them.
Ithamore. How so?
Barabas. Belike there is some ceremony in 't.   85
   There, Ithamore, must thou go place this pot.
   Stay, let me spice it first.
Ithamore. Pray do, and let me help you, master. Pray let me
   taste first.
Barabas. Prithee do. [*Ithamore tastes.*] What say'st thou now?   90
Ithamore. Troth, master, I'm loath such a pot of pottage
   should be spoiled.
Barabas. [*Putting in poison*]
   Peace, Ithamore. 'Tis better so than spared.

---

66. *mess*] portion.

68. *batten*] fatten, nourish.

77–8.] Every year on this evening (St Jacques' Eve), the Maltese make it
a practice.

80. *Among the rest*] along with others who are taking alms (charitable gifts)
to the nunnery.

93. *'Tis . . . spared*] It will be better so than if we tried to save the pottage
for eating.

Assure thyself thou shalt have broth by the eye.

My purse, my coffer, and myself is thine.   95

Ithamore. Well, master, I go.   [*He starts to go.*]

Barabas. Stay, first let me stir it, Ithamore.

As fatal be it to her as the draught

Of which great Alexander drunk and died!

And with her let it work like Borgia's wine,   100

Whereof his sire, the Pope, was poisonèd!

In few, the blood of Hydra, Lerna's bane,

The juice of hebon, and Cocytus' breath,

And all the poisons of the Stygian pool,

Break from the fiery kingdom, and in this   105

Vomit your venom, and envenom her

That like a fiend hath left her father thus!

Ithamore. [*Aside*] *What a blessing has he given 't! Was ever pot of rice-porridge so sauced?*—What shall I do with it?

Barabas. O my sweet Ithamore, go set it down,   110

And come again so soon as thou hast done,

For I have other business for thee.

Ithamore. Here's a drench to poison a whole stable of Flanders mares. I'll carry it to the nuns with a powder.

Barabas. And the horse-pestilence to boot. Away!   115

---

94. *by the eye*] as much as your eye desires.

99. *Alexander*] According to an inaccurate legend, Alexander the Great was given poisoned wine by Antipater. He died in 323 B.C., probably of a fever.

100. *like Borgia's wine*] In a similarly erroneous account, Pope Alexander VI (Rodrigo Borgia) was supposed to have died accidentally in 1503 through drinking poisoned wine that his son, Cesare Borgia, had prepared for other victims.

102. *In few*] in short.

Hydra] One of Hercules's twelve labours was to kill the Lernean Hydra, a monstrous water-snake with poisonous blood.

103. *hebon*] a poison, associated with ebony, yew, henbane, and hemlock.

Cocytus] the river of lamentation in the underworld.

104. *Stygian pool*] Styx was the principal river of the underworld.

113. *drench*] dose of medicine given to an animal.

114. *Flanders mares*] (1) horses with a reputation for being difficult to control; (2) lascivious women.

with a powder] in great haste (punning on 'powder' as a term for a poisonous dose).

115.] i.e. 'and put in some terrible disease in addition. Get going!' (with a hidden suggestion also that Barabas wishes a plague on Ithamore).

Ithamore. I am gone.
    Pay me my wages, for my work is done.
                            Exit [*with the pot*].
Barabas. I'll pay thee with a vengeance, Ithamore.   *Exit.*

[III. v]

    Enter FERNEZE, [MARTIN DEL] BOSCO, Knights [*and*] Bashaw.

Ferneze. Welcome, great bashaw. How fares Calymath?
    What wind drives you thus into Malta road?
Bashaw. The wind that bloweth all the world besides:
    Desire of gold.
Ferneze.   Desire of gold, great sir?
    That's to be gotten in the Western Ind.   5
    In Malta are no golden minerals.
Bashaw. To you of Malta thus saith Calymath:
    The time you took for respite is at hand
    For the performance of your promise passed,
    And for the tribute-money I am sent.   10
Ferneze. Bashaw, in brief, shalt have no tribute here,
    Nor shall the heathens live upon our spoil.
    First will we raze the city walls ourselves,
    Lay waste the island, hew the temples down,
    And, shipping off our goods to Sicily,   15
    Open an entrance for the wasteful sea,
    Whose billows, beating the resistless banks,
    Shall overflow it with their refluence.
Bashaw. Well, governor, since thou hast broke the league
    By flat denial of the promised tribute,   20

---

118. *pay*] (1) give money to; (2) settle accounts with.
with a vengeance] (1) with a curse; (2) to an extreme degree.

III.v.5. *Western Ind*] i.e. the West 'Indies', America, especially the gold
and silver mines of Central and South America.
  9. *passed*] (1) duly made or given; (2) past (the Q spelling).
 11. *shalt*] thou shalt.
 12. *live . . . spoil*] i.e. gain wealth from sacking our city.
 16. *wasteful*] causing devastation and ruin.
 17. *resistless*] unresisting.
 18. *refluence*] flowing back, reflux.

Talk not of razing down your city walls;
You shall not need trouble yourselves so far,
For Selim Calymath shall come himself,
And with brass bullets batter down your towers,
And turn proud Malta to a wilderness   25
For these intolerable wrongs of yours;
And so farewell.
Ferneze. Farewell.   [*Exit* Bashaw.]
And now, you men of Malta, look about,
And let's provide to welcome Calymath.   30
Close your portcullis, charge your basilisks,
And as you profitably take up arms,
So now courageously encounter them;
For by this answer, broken is the league,
And naught is to be looked for now but wars,   35
And naught to us more welcome is than wars.   *Exeunt.*

[III. vi]

Enter the two friars [JACOMO *and* Friar BERNARDINE].

Jacomo. Oh, brother, brother, all the nuns are sick,
And physic will not help them; they must die.
Bernardine. The abbess sent for me to be confessed.
Oh, what a sad confession will there be!
Jacomo. And so did fair Maria send for me.   5
I'll to her lodging; hereabouts she lies.   *Exit.*

Enter ABIGAIL.

Bernardine. What, all dead save only Abigail?
Abigail. And I shall die too, for I feel death coming.
Where is the friar that conversed with me?
Bernardine. Oh, he is gone to see the other nuns.   10

---

31. *portcullis*] heavy grated gateway.
basilisks] large cannons, generally made of brass.
32. *profitably*] (1) in a worthy cause; (2) with hope of financial gain.

III.vi.2. *physic*] medicine.
6. *lies*] dwells. (But the passage is filled with sexual suggestion.)
9.] For the conversation of Abigail and Jacomo, see III.iii.59–82.

Abigail. I sent for him, but, seeing you are come,
    Be you my ghostly father; and first know
    That in this house I lived religiously,
    Chaste, and devout, much sorrowing for my sins;
    But ere I came—   15
Bernardine. What then?
Abigail. I did offend high heaven so grievously
    As I am almost desperate for my sins;
    And one offence torments me more than all.
    You knew Mathias and Don Lodowick?   20
Bernardine. Yes, what of them?
Abigail. My father did contract me to 'em both:
    First to Don Lodowick—him I never loved;
    Mathias was the man that I held dear,
    And for his sake did I become a nun.   25
Bernardine. So; say how was their end?
Abigail. Both, jealous of my love, envied each other;
    And by my father's practice, which is there
    Set down at large, the gallants were both slain.
                       [She gives a paper.]
Bernardine. Oh, monstrous villainy!   30
Abigail. To work my peace, this I confess to thee.
    Reveal it not, for then my father dies.
Bernardine. Know that confession must not be revealed;
    The canon law forbids it, and the priest
    That makes it known, being degraded first,   35
    Shall be condemned and then sent to the fire.
Abigail. So I have heard; pray therefore keep it close.
    Death seizeth on my heart. Ah, gentle friar,

---

12. *ghostly father*] spiritual father, confessor.
18. *desperate*] in the theological sense, 'without hope of salvation'.
22. *contract*] betroth.
27. *envied*] showed ill-will or malice towards; were jealous towards. (Accented on the second syllable.)
28. *practice*] scheming.
29. *at large*] at length, in full.
31. *work my peace*] achieve peace of mind and spirit.
35. *degraded*] deprived of orders.
36.] (An exaggeration; priests might be defrocked and even excommunicated for disclosing what they heard in confession, but not executed.)

Convert my father that he may be saved,
And witness that I die a Christian!   [*She dies.*]   40
Bernardine. Ay, and a virgin, too: that grieves me most.
But I must to the Jew and exclaim on him,
And make him stand in fear of me.

Enter Friar JACOMO.

Jacomo. Oh, brother, all the nuns are dead! Let's bury them.
Bernardine. First help to bury this; then go with me,   45
And help me to exclaim against the Jew.
Jacomo. Why, what has he done?
Bernardine. A thing that makes me tremble to unfold.
Jacomo. What, has he crucified a child?
Bernardine. No, but a worse thing. 'Twas told me in shrift;   50
Thou know'st 'tis death an if it be revealed.
Come, let's away.   *Exeunt [with the body].*

41.] i.e. (1) 'it grieves me most that a young maiden should die'; (2) 'it
grieves me that she was not sexually enjoyed'.

42. *exclaim on*] accuse, cry out against.

49. *has . . . child*] Wild anti-Semitic fantasies were common in medieval
and Renaissance Europe of Jews kidnapping and crucifying children, and
similar supposed atrocities.

50. *shrift*] confession.

51. *an if*] if.

Act IV

[IV. i]

Enter BARABAS [*and*] ITHAMORE. *Bells within.*

Barabas. There is no music to a Christian's knell.
    How sweet the bells ring, now the nuns are dead,
    That sound at other times like tinkers' pans!
    I was afraid the poison had not wrought,
    Or, though it wrought, it would have done no good,   5
    For every year they swell, and yet they live.
    Now all are dead; not one remains alive.
Ithamore. That's brave, master, but think you it will not be
    known?
Barabas. How can it if we two be secret?   10
Ithamore. For my part fear you not.
Barabas. I'd cut thy throat if I did.
Ithamore. And reason too.
    But here's a royal monastery hard by;
    Good master, let me poison all the monks.   15
Barabas. Thou shalt not need, for, now the nuns are dead,
    They'll die with grief.
Ithamore. Do you not sorrow for your daughter's death?
Barabas. No, but I grieve because she lived so long.

IV.i.1. *to*] compared to.

    4. *wrought*] worked, taken effect.

    6. *swell*] grow round in pregnancy. The grisly joke is that the nuns' bodies, swollen with poison, will resemble those of pregnant women.

    8. *brave*] splendid.

    13. *reason*] with reason, rightly.

    14. *royal*] first-class.

    17. *They*] the monks. The coarse suggestion is that the monks have all been sleeping with the nuns, and so will grieve.

An Hebrew born, and would become a Christian!   20
Catzo, diavola!

Enter the two friars [JACOMO *and* BERNARDINE].

Ithamore. Look, look, master, here come two religious
    caterpillars.
Barabas. I smelt 'em ere they came.
Ithamore. [*Aside*] *God-a-mercy, nose!*—Come, let's be gone.   25
Bernardine. Stay, wicked Jew! Repent, I say, and stay.
Jacomo. Thou hast offended, therefore must be damned.
Barabas. [*Aside to Ithamore*]
    I fear they know we sent the poisoned broth.
Ithamore. [*Aside*] *And so do I, master. Therefore, speak 'em
    fair.*   30
Bernardine. Barabas, thou hast—
Jacomo. Ay, that thou hast—
Barabas. True, I have money; what though I have?
Bernardine. Thou art a—
Jacomo. Ay, that thou art, a—   35
Barabas. What needs all this? I know I am a Jew.
Bernardine. Thy daughter—
Jacomo. Ay, thy daughter—
Barabas. Oh, speak not of her, then I die with grief.
Bernardine. Remember that—   40
Jacomo. Ay, remember that—
Barabas. I must needs say that I have been a great usurer.
Bernardine. Thou hast committed—
Barabas.   Fornication?
    But that was in another country,
    And besides, the wench is dead.   45
Bernardine. Ay, but Barabas, remember Mathias and Don
    Lodowick.

---

21. Catzo, diavola] i.e. 'Damn! What a devil she is!' *Catzo* is, literally,
Italian slang for 'penis'.

23. *caterpillars*] i.e. (1) creatures dressed in friars' woolly black robes,
resembling caterpillars; (2) extortioners that prey upon society.

25. God-a-mercy, nose!] i.e. 'Praise God for such a magnificent nose that
can smell out rascals!' Compare II.iii.176 and III.iii.10.

31–43.] The rapid-fire speeches and the repetitions suggest that the two
friars are speaking almost simultaneously and interrupting each other.

Barabas. Why, what of them?
Bernardine. I will not say that by a forged challenge they met.
Barabas. [*Aside*] *She has confessed, and we are both undone.*   50
    My bosom inmates!—(*Aside*) *but I must dissemble.*—
    O holy friars, the burden of my sins
    Lie heavy on my soul. Then pray you tell me,
    Is 't not too late now to turn Christian?
    I have been zealous in the Jewish faith,   55
    Hard-hearted to the poor, a covetous wretch,
    That would for lucre's sake have sold my soul.
    A hundred for a hundred I have ta'en,
    And now for store of wealth may I compare
    With all the Jews in Malta. But what is wealth?   60
    I am a Jew, and therefore am I lost.
    Would penance serve for this my sin,
    I could afford to whip myself to death—
Ithamore. [*Aside*] *And so could I; but penance will not serve—*
Barabas. To fast, to pray, and wear a shirt of hair,   65
    And on my knees creep to Jerusalem.
    Cellars of wine and sollars full of wheat,
    Warehouses stuffed with spices and with drugs,
    Whole chests of gold, in bullion and in coin,
    Besides I know not how much weight in pearl,   70
    Orient and round, have I within my house;
    At Alexandria, merchandise unsold.
    But yesterday two ships went from this town;
    Their voyage will be worth ten thousand crowns.
    In Florence, Venice, Antwerp, London, Seville,   75
    Frankfurt, Lubeck, Moscow, and where not,
    Have I debts owing, and, in most of these,
    Great sums of money lying in the banco.

---

53. *Lie*] a plural verb following a plural concept: 'the burden of my sins'.
58.] 'I have taken a hundred per cent interest.'
61. *lost*] spiritually lost, damned.
64.] Perhaps in a comic aside, Ithamore comments on the ridiculous idea
of Barabas's whipping himself to death to benefit his soul.
67. *sollars*] lofts or attics, used as storerooms.
71. *Orient*] lustrous, precious.
72. *unsold*] not yet sold for profit. (*Untold* is a possible emendation.)
73. *But*] only.
78. *banco*] bank.

All this I'll give to some religious house,
So I may be baptized and live therein.   80
Jacomo. Oh, good Barabas, come to our house!
Bernardine. Oh, no, good Barabas, come to our house!
And Barabas, you know—
Barabas. [*To Bernardine*] I know that I have highly sinned.
You shall convert me; you shall have all my wealth.   85
Jacomo. Oh, Barabas, their laws are strict.
Barabas. [*To Jacomo*]
I know they are, and I will be with you.
Jacomo. They wear no shirts, and they go barefoot too.
Barabas. [*To Jacomo*] Then 'tis not for me; and I am resolved
You shall confess me, and have all my goods.   90
Bernardine. Good Barabas, come to me.
Barabas. [*To Jacomo*]
You see I answer him, and yet he stays.
Rid him away, and go you home with me.
Jacomo. [*To Barabas*] I'll be with you tonight.
Barabas. [*To Jacomo*]
Come to my house at one o'clock this night.   95
Jacomo. [*To Bernardine*]
You hear your answer, and you may be gone.
Bernardine. Why, go get you away.
Jacomo. I will not go for thee.
Bernardine. Not? Then I'll make thee, rogue.
Jacomo. How, dost call me rogue?   [*They*] *fight.*   100
Ithamore. Part 'em, master, part 'em.
Barabas. This is mere frailty. Brethren, be content.
Friar Bernardine, go you with Ithamore.

---

80. *So*] provided.
81–112.] Barabas tantalizes the friars by pretending to auction himself off
to the highest bidder.
93. *Rid . . . away*] get rid of him, remove him.
98. *for thee*] at your bidding.
99. *thee, rogue*] Q's 'thee goe' may be a compositorial mistake. The passage shows some textual confusion. This edition reassigns l. 91 from Friar
'1.', normally Jacomo, to Bernardine, and l. 94 from '2.' to Jacomo; similarly,
ll. 104–5, assigned to *Ith.* in Q, are reassigned here to Bernardine (l. 104) and
Jacomo (l. 105).

[*Aside to Bernardine*]
You know my mind; let me alone with him.

Jacomo. Why does he go to thy house? Let him be gone.   105

Barabas. [*Aside to Bernardine*]
I'll give him something, and so stop his mouth.

Exeunt [ITHAMORE *and* BERNARDINE].

I never heard of any man but he
Maligned the order of the Jacobins.
But do you think that I believe his words?
Why, brother, you converted Abigail,   110
And I am bound in charity to requite it;
And so I will. O Jacomo, fail not, but come!

Jacomo. But Barabas, who shall be your godfathers?
For presently you shall be shrived.

Barabas. Marry, the Turk shall be one of my godfathers,   115
But not a word to any of your convent.

Jacomo. I warrant thee, Barabas.   *Exit.*

Barabas. So, now the fear is past, and I am safe,
For he that shrived her is within my house.
What if I murdered him ere Jacomo comes?   120
Now I have such a plot for both their lives
As never Jew nor Christian knew the like.
One turned my daughter, therefore he shall die;
The other knows enough to have my life,
Therefore 'tis not requisite he should live.   125
But are not both these wise men to suppose
That I will leave my house, my goods, and all,
To fast and be well whipped? I'll none of that.

---

104. *let . . . him*] leave me to deal with him.
107. *he*] Bernardine.
108. *Jacobins*] Dominicans or black friars, as at III.iii.32.
111. *requite*] charitably repay (but with hidden meaning of 'revenge').
114. *shrived*] confessed, given absolution.
115. *Marry*] an oath, originally 'by the Virgin Mary'.
the Turk] i.e. Ithamore.
117. *warrant*] assure.
119. *he . . . her*] Bernardine. See III.vi.12–32.
123. *One*] Jacomo.
turned] converted.
124. *The other*] Bernardine.
125.] 'Therefore it is requisite that he not live.'

Now, Friar Bernardine, I come to you.
I'll feast you, lodge you, give you fair words,   130
And after that, I and my trusty Turk—
No more but so. It must and shall be done.

Enter ITHAMORE.

Ithamore, tell me, is the friar asleep?
Ithamore. Yes; and I know not what the reason is,
    Do what I can he will not strip himself,   135
    Nor go to bed, but sleeps in his own clothes.
    I fear me he mistrusts what we intend.
Barabas. No, 'tis an order which the friars use.
    Yet if he knew our meanings, could he 'scape?
Ithamore. No, none can hear him, cry he ne'er so loud.   140
Barabas. Why, true, therefore did I place him there.
    The other chambers open towards the street.
Ithamore. You loiter, master. Wherefore stay we thus?
    Oh, how I long to see him shake his heels!
       [*He draws curtains, revealing* BERNARDINE *asleep.*]
Barabas. Come on, sirrah: 145
    Off with your girdle, make a handsome noose.
    Friar, awake! [*He puts the noose round Bernardine's neck.*]
Bernardine. What, do you mean to strangle me?
Ithamore. Yes, 'cause you use to confess.
Barabas. Blame not us but the proverb, 'confess and be   150
    hanged'.—Pull hard.

---

132. *No . . . so*] i.e. 'without more ado'.
138. *order*] religious observance.
139. *if*] even if.
143. *Wherefore stay we*] why do we hesitate.
144. *shake his heels*] i.e. dangle at the end of a rope.
144.1.] This action may use a 'discovery space' rearstage in the Elizabethan playhouse, here imagined to be Barabas's house even though the scene began elsewhere.
146.] Barabas addresses the still sleeping Bernardine, as the friar's girdle is slipped off him to serve as a noose.
149. *use to confess*] make a practice of hearing confession (and thus knew too much; besides, any Catholic friar deserves death in Ithamore's view).
150–1.] Barabas sardonically cites a proverb to express his agreement with Ithamore, even though the proverb does not really apply to a religious confession.

Bernardine. What, will you have my life?
Barabas. Pull hard, I say!—You would have had my goods.
Ithamore. Ay, and our lives too; therefore pull amain.

                                             [They strangle him.]

    'Tis neatly done, sir. Here's no print at all.   155
Barabas. Then is it as it should be. Take him up.
Ithamore. Nay, master, be ruled by me a little. *[He stands up*
    the body.] So, let him lean upon his staff. Excellent! He
    stands as if he were begging of bacon.
Barabas. Who would not think but that this friar lived?   160
    What time o' night is 't now, sweet Ithamore?
Ithamore. Towards one.
Barabas. Then will not Jacomo be long from hence.

                                        [They conceal themselves.]

                Enter [Friar] JACOMO.

Jacomo. This is the hour wherein I shall proceed.
    Oh, happy hour,   165
    Wherein I shall convert an infidel
    And bring his gold into our treasury!
    But soft, is not this Bernardine? It is;
    And, understanding I should come this way,
    Stands here o' purpose, meaning me some wrong,   170
    And intercepts my going to the Jew.—
    Bernardine!
    Wilt thou not speak? Thou think'st I see thee not.
    Away, I'd wish thee, and let me go by.
    No, wilt thou not? Nay then, I'll force my way;   175
    And see, a staff stands ready for the purpose.

---

  152. *have*] Q's 'saue' doesn't make sense.
  154. *amain*] violently, with all one's might.
  155. *print*] mark from the noose.
  157–63.] We are now to imagine the action as taking place outside
Barabas's house, where Barabas and Ithamore can conceal themselves to spy
on Jacomo's arrival. They may simply come forward from hiding at l. 177.2,
where Q specifies that they *Enter*.
  164. *proceed*] make progress, prosper.
  176. *a staff*] Quite possibly, Jacomo grabs the staff used at ll. 157–8 to
prop up the dead Bernardine, and quickly strikes Jacomo as he falls, not
realizing how he has been tricked.

As thou likest that, stop me another time.

Strike[s] him; he falls.

Enter BARABAS [*and* ITHAMORE *from concealment*].

Barabas. Why, how now, Jacomo, what hast thou done?

Jacomo. Why, stricken him that would have struck at me.

Barabas. Who is it? Bernardine? Now out, alas, he is slain!   180

Ithamore. Ay, master, he's slain. Look how his brains drop out
    on 's nose.

Jacomo. Good sirs, I have done 't, but nobody knows it but
    you two, I may escape.

Barabas. So might my man and I hang with you for company.   185

Ithamore. No, let us bear him to the magistrates.

Jacomo. Good Barabas, let me go.

Barabas. No, pardon me, the law must have his course.
    I must be forced to give in evidence
    That, being importuned by this Bernardine   190
    To be a Christian, I shut him out,
    And there he sat. Now I, to keep my word,
    And give my goods and substance to your house,
    Was up thus early, with intent to go
    Unto your friary, because you stayed.   195

Ithamore. Fie upon 'em, master, will you turn Christian, when
    holy friars turn devils and murder one another?

Barabas. No; for this example I'll remain a Jew.
    Heaven bless me! What, a friar a murderer?
    When shall you see a Jew commit the like?   200

Ithamore. Why, a Turk could ha' done no more.

Barabas. Tomorrow is the sessions; you shall to it.
    Come, Ithamore, let's help to take him hence.

Jacomo. Villains, I am a sacred person. Touch me not.

---

180. *out*] an expression of dismay.
182. *on 's*] of his.
188. *his*] its.
189. *give in evidence*] testify.
195. *stayed*] were waiting for me, or were late in coming.
198. *for this example*] because of this instance (of the friars' evil ways).
202. *sessions*] law-court sessions.

Barabas. The law shall touch you; we'll but lead you, we.   205
  'Las, I could weep at your calamity.
  Take in the staff too, for that must be shown;
  Law wills that each particular be known.   *Exeunt.*

[IV. ii]

   Enter Courtesan [BELLAMIRA] *and* PILIA-BORZA.

Bellamira. Pilia-Borza, didst thou meet with Ithamore?
Pilia-Borza. I did.
Bellamira. And didst thou deliver my letter?
Pilia-Borza. I did.
Bellamira. And what think'st thou, will he come?   5
Pilia-Borza. I think so, and yet I cannot tell, for at the reading
  of the letter he looked like a man of another world.
Bellamira. Why so?
Pilia-Borza. That such a base slave as he should be saluted by
  such a tall man as I am, from such a beautiful dame as   10
  you.
Bellamira. And what said he?
Pilia-Borza. Not a wise word; only gave me a nod, as who
  should say, 'Is it even so?'; and so I left him, being driven
  to a non-plus at the critical aspect of my terrible   15
  countenance.
Bellamira. And where didst meet him?

---

 205. *touch*] censure, handle, vex, sting (with wordplay on *Touch*, physically contact, in l. 204. 'Touch me not' is also a blasphemous recollection of Christ's answer ('*Noli me tangere*') to Mary Magdalene when he encounters her after his resurrection; see John, 20.17).
 208. *wills*] requires, decrees.

 IV.ii.7. *a man . . . world*] a ghost or spirit (pale with fear).
 9. *saluted*] greeted.
 10. *tall*] brave.
 13–14. *as . . . so?*] as if one were to say, 'Is that how it is?'
 15. *non-plus*] state of bewilderment.
 critical aspect] (1) sinister astrological influence of the planets; (2) daunting expression; (3) censorious look.

Pilia-Borza. Upon mine own freehold, within forty foot of the
gallows, conning his neck-verse, I take it, looking of a
friar's execution, whom I saluted with an old hempen   20
proverb, '*hodie tibi, cras mihi*', and so I left him to the
mercy of the hangman; but the exercise being done, see
where he comes.

Enter ITHAMORE.

Ithamore. [*To himself*] I never knew a man take his death so
patiently as this friar. He was ready to leap off ere the   25
halter was about his neck, and, when the hangman had
put on his hempen tippet, he made such haste to his
prayers as if he had had another cure to serve. Well, go
whither he will, I'll be none of his followers in hastè. And
now I think on 't, going to the execution, a fellow met me   30
with a muschatoes like a raven's wing and a dagger with
a hilt like a warming-pan, and he gave me a letter from
one Madam Bellamira, saluting me in such sort as if he
had meant to make clean my boots with his lips; the effect
was, that I should come to her house. I wonder what the   35
reason is; it may be she sees more in me than I can find
in myself, for she writes further that she loves me ever
since she saw me, and who would not requite such love?
Here's her house, and here she comes, and now would I
were gone! I am not worthy to look upon her.   40

18–20. *Upon . . . execution*] i.e. 'on my own terrain, around the gallows
(where I pick pockets of the crowd watching public hangings), while he was
trying to memorize the fifty-first psalm (*Misereri mei*, etc.) that would entitle
him to claim benefit of clergy and thus save his life if he were caught, and was
witnessing the execution of Friar Jacomo'.

20. *whom*] i.e. Ithamore.

hempen] (1) homespun; (2) well suited to the gallows, with its noose made
of hemp.

21. hodie . . . mihi] 'Your turn today, mine tomorrow.'

22. *exercise*] Pilia-Borza speaks sardonically as though the hanging were an
exercise or religious ceremony.

27. *hempen tippet*] i.e. noose. A *tippet* is a neck-band on a priest's robe.

28. *cure*] cure of souls, parish.

31. *muschatoes*] pair of moustaches.

32. *warming-pan*] long-handled pan filled with hot water to heat a bed,
grotesquely resembling a fat-handled dagger.

34. *effect*] purport, gist.

Pilia-Borza. [*To Bellamira*] This is the gentleman you writ
  to.
Ithamore. [*Aside*] '*Gentleman*'! *He flouts me. What gentry can
  be in a poor Turk of tenpence? I'll be gone.*
Bellamira. Is 't not a sweet-faced youth, Pilia?   45
Ithamore. [*Aside*] *Again, 'sweet youth'!*—Did not you, sir,
  bring the sweet youth a letter?
Pilia-Borza. I did, sir, and from this gentlewoman, who, as
  myself and the rest of the family, stand or fall at your
  service.   50
Bellamira. Though woman's modesty should hale me back,
  I can withhold no longer. Welcome, sweet love.
Ithamore. [*Aside*] *Now am I clean, or rather foully, out of the
  way.*   [*He starts to leave.*]
Bellamira. Whither so soon?   55
Ithamore. [*Aside*] *I'll go steal some money from my master to
  make me handsome.*—Pray pardon me. I must go see a
  ship discharged.
Bellamira. Canst thou be so unkind to leave me thus?
Pilia-Borza. An ye did but know how she loves you, sir!   60
Ithamore. Nay, I care not how much she loves me.—Sweet
  Bellamira, would I had my master's wealth for thy sake.
Pilia-Borza. And you can have it, sir, an if you please.
Ithamore. If 'twere above ground I could and would have it,
  but he hides and buries it up as partridges do their eggs,   65
  under the earth.

---

43. flouts] mocks.
  gentry] rank of gentleman.
44. Turk of tenpence] almost penniless rogue.
49. *family*] members of the household (with the implication that they are
Ithamore's servants).
  stand or fall] (1) prosper or languish; (2) become erect or detumescent; (3)
stand awaiting your orders, or submit to you sexually by lying down.
51. *hale*] pull, hold.
52. *withhold*] hold back.
53. clean] 'wholly'; but Ithamore plays on the sense of 'not dirty', as
opposed to *foul*.
53-4. out of the way] going in the wrong direction, following the wrong
course of action. (Ithamore is so infatuated with Bellamira that he thinks he
is not 'up' to encountering her.)
58. *discharged*] unloaded.
60. *An*] if.

Pilia-Borza. And is 't not possible to find it out?

Ithamore. By no means possible.

Bellamira. [*Aside to Pilia-Borza*]
    What shall we do with this base villain, then?

Pilia-Borza. [*To Bellamira*]
    Let me alone. Do but you speak him fair.—   70
    But you know some secrets of the Jew,
    Which if they were revealed would do him harm.

Ithamore. Ay, and such as—Go to, no more, I'll make him
    send me half he has, and glad he 'scapes so too. Pen and
    ink! I'll write unto him. We'll have money straight.   75

Pilia-Borza. Send for a hundred crowns at least.

Ithamore. Ten hundred thousand crowns. (*He writes.*) 'Master
    Barabas—'

Pilia-Borza. Write not so submissively, but threatening him.

Ithamore. 'Sirrah Barabas, send me a hundred crowns.'   80

Pilia-Borza. Put in two hundred at least.

Ithamore. 'I charge thee send me three hundred by this
    bearer, and this shall be your warrant. If you do not, no
    more but so.'

Pilia-Borza. Tell him you will confess.   85

Ithamore. 'Otherwise I'll confess all.'—Vanish, and return in a
    twinkle.

Pilia-Borza. Let me alone. I'll use him in his kind.   [*Exit.*]

Ithamore. Hang him, Jew!

Bellamira. Now, gentle Ithamore, lie in my lap.   90
    Where are my maids? Provide a running banquet.
    Send to the merchant; bid him bring me silks.
    Shall Ithamore my love go in such rags?

---

70. Let me alone] leave it to me.
speak him fair] flatter him.

73. *Go to*] an expression of impatience or expostulation.

80. *Sirrah*] used to address a social inferior or servant, here used as a deliberate insubordination.

83. *warrant*] writ authorizing the delivery of the money.

83–4. *no more but so*] i.e. you'll suffer the consequences.

88. *use . . . kind*] (1) treat him as his nature deserves; (2) treat him as a Jew, i.e. harshly.

90. *lie in my lap*] Hamlet's offer to lie with his head in Ophelia's lap (*Hamlet*, III.ii.110–14) has a similarly sexual suggestiveness.

91. *running banquet*] light meal or snack. (It is probably not brought onstage.)

Ithamore. And bid the jeweller come hither too.

Bellamira. I have no husband, sweet; I'll marry thee.   95

Ithamore. Content, but we will leave this paltry land
    And sail from hence to Greece, to lovely Greece.
    I'll be thy Jason, thou my golden fleece.
    Where painted carpets o'er the meads are hurled
    And Bacchus' vineyards overspread the world,   100
    Where woods and forests go in goodly green,
    I'll be Adonis, thou shalt be Love's Queen.
    The meads, the orchards, and the primrose lanes,
    Instead of sedge and reed, bear sugar-canes.
    Thou in those groves, by Dis above,   105
    Shalt live with me and be my love.

Bellamira. Whither will I not go with gentle Ithamore?

Enter PILIA-BORZA.

Ithamore. How now? Hast thou the gold?

Pilia-Borza. Yes.

Ithamore. But came it freely? Did the cow give down her milk   110
    freely?

Pilia-Borza. At reading of the letter, he stared and stamped
    and turned aside; I took him by the beard, and looked
    upon him thus, told him he were best to send it; then he
    hugged and embraced me.   115

Ithamore. Rather for fear than love.

Pilia-Borza. Then like a Jew he laughed and jeered, and told
    me he loved me for your sake, and said what a faithful
    servant you had been.

---

96. *Content*] agreed.

98. *golden fleece*] Ithamore conjures up the heroic tale of the Argonauts' voyage only to undercut it with a sardonic suggestion of 'fleecing' or plundering.

99. *painted carpets*] a carpeting of brightly coloured flowers.

102. *Love's Queen*] Venus, the goddess of love, fell in love with a beautiful young man, Adonis, with tragic consequences (Ovid, *Metamorphoses*).

105. *Dis*] the Roman god of the underworld, equivalent of Pluto or Hades. His kingdom is below, not 'above'. Ithamore may mean something like 'by almighty Dis'.

113. *took . . . beard*] a very insulting gesture.

114. *thus*] (The actor makes a ferocious face.)
he were best] he would be well advised.

Ithamore. The more villain he to keep me thus. Here's goodly   120
'parel, is there not?
Pilia-Borza. To conclude, he gave me ten crowns.
Ithamore. But ten? I'll not leave him worth a grey groat. Give
me a ream of paper; we'll have a kingdom of gold for 't.
Pilia-Borza. Write for five hundred crowns.   125
Ithamore. [*Writes.*] 'Sirrah Jew, as you love your life send me
five hundred crowns, and give the bearer a hundred.' Tell
him I must have 't.
Pilia-Borza. I warrant your worship shall have 't.
Ithamore. And if he ask why I demand so much, tell him I   130
scorn to write a line under a hundred crowns.
Pilia-Borza. You'd make a rich poet, sir. I am gone.   *Exit.*
Ithamore. [*To Bellamira*]
Take thou the money. Spend it for my sake.
Bellamira. 'Tis not thy money but thyself I weigh.
Thus Bellamira esteems of gold—   [*She throws it aside.*]   135
But thus of thee.   *Kiss[es] him.*
Ithamore. [*Aside*] *That kiss again! She runs division of my lips.*
What an eye she casts on me! It twinkles like a star.
Bellamira. Come, my dear love, let's in and sleep together.
Ithamore. Oh, that ten thousand nights were put in one, that   140
we might sleep seven years together afore we wake!
Bellamira. Come, amorous wag, first banquet and then sleep.
[*Exeunt.*]

120–1. *Here's . . . not?*] i.e. 'How do you like the rags that serve as my
apparel? That's all he provides me.'

122. *ten crowns*] It appears from IV.iii.18–20 that Barabas handed over the
full amount of three hundred crowns, so this must be a tip for Pilia-Borza.

123. *grey groat*] a small silver coin worth fourpence.

124. *ream*] (1) large quantity of paper, usually 480–500 sheets; (2) realm
(playing on *kingdom*), often pronounced in Elizabethan English without the
'l' sound.

127. *a hundred*] i.e. as a tip; see l. 122 and note.

131. *write . . . under*] write a letter demanding anything less than.

137. division] a musical term, meaning the dividing of long notes into
short notes, and hence the execution of an elaborate variation or descant on
a theme. Bellamira is a virtuoso in the art of kissing.

142. *wag*] an affectionate term for a somewhat mischievous or impudent
young man.

[IV. iii]

Enter BARABAS *reading [Ithamore's first] letter.*

Barabas. 'Barabas, send me three hundred crowns.'
    Plain 'Barabas'. Oh, that wicked courtesan!
    He was not wont to call me Barabas.
    'Or else I will confess.' Ay, there it goes.
    But if I get him, *coupe de gorge* for that!   5
    He sent a shaggy tattered staring slave,
    That when he speaks draws out his grisly beard
    And winds it twice or thrice about his ear;
    Whose face has been a grindstone for men's swords;
    His hands are hacked, some fingers cut quite off;   10
    Who, when he speaks, grunts like a hog, and looks
    Like one that is employed in catzerie
    And crossbiting; such a rogue
    As is the husband to a hundred whores—
    And I by him must send three hundred crowns!   15
    Well, my hope is he will not stay there still;
    And when he comes—Oh, that he were but here!

Enter PILIA-BORZA.

Pilia-Borza. Jew, I must ha' more gold.
Barabas. Why, want'st thou any of thy tale?
Pilia-Borza. No; but three hundred will not serve his turn.   20
Barabas. Not serve his turn, sir?
Pilia-Borza. No, sir; and therefore I must have five hundred
    more.
Barabas. I'll rather—

  IV.iii.3. *wont*] accustomed.
    5. coupe de gorge] i.e. 'I'll cut his throat'.
    6. *slave*] rogue (Pilia-Borza).
    12. *catzerie*] roguery. (See IV.i.21 and note.)
    13. *crossbiting*] swindling, outwitting in trickery.
    13–14. *such . . . whores*] a pimp who pretends to be husband to whores in
order to blackmail their clients.
    16. *he*] Ithamore.
  still] for ever, for good.
    19.] 'Why, is anything missing from the total amount you should have?'
    20. *serve his turn*] with suggestion of 'provide for his sexual pleasure'.

Pilia-Borza. Oh, good words, sir; and send it, you were best.   25
    See, there's his letter.
                        [He presents Ithamore's second letter.]
Barabas. Might he not as well come as send? Pray bid him
    come and fetch it. What he writes for you, ye shall have
    straight.
Pilia-Borza. Ay, and the rest too, or else—   30
Barabas. [*Aside*] *I must make this villain away.*—Please you
    dine with me, sir; and you shall be most heartily *poisoned.*
                                  (Aside.)
Pilia-Borza. No, God-a-mercy. Shall I have these crowns?
Barabas. I cannot do it. I have lost my keys.
Pilia-Borza. Oh, if that be all, I can pick ope your locks.   35
Barabas. Or climb up to my counting-house window? You
    know my meaning.
Pilia-Borza. I know enough, and therefore talk not to me of
    your counting-house. The gold, or know, Jew, it is in my
    power to hang thee.   40
Barabas. [*Aside*] *I am betrayed.*—
    'Tis not five hundred crowns that I esteem,
    I am not moved at that; this angers me,
    That he who knows I love him as myself
    Should write in this imperious vein. Why, sir,   45
    You know I have no child, and unto whom
    Should I leave all but unto Ithamore?
Pilia-Borza. Here's many words, but no crowns. The crowns!
Barabas. Commend me to him, sir, most humbly,
    And unto your good mistress as unknown.   50
Pilia-Borza. Speak, shall I have 'em, sir?
Barabas. Sir, here they are.   *[He gives money.]*
    [*Aside*] *Oh, that I should part with so much gold!*
    Here, take 'em, fellow, with as good a will—
    As I would see thee hanged. Oh, love stops my breath.   55

---

    25. *good words*] i.e. speak calmly.
    28. *it*] i.e. the hundred crowns as a tip for the bearer; see IV.ii.125–7.
    31. make . . . away] do away with this rogue.
    36–7.] Barabas knows or suspects how Pilia-Borza climbed up with hooks
to Barabas's counting house; see III.i.18–23.
    50. *as unknown*] whom I have not met.

Never loved man servant as I do Ithamore.

Pilia-Borza. I know it, sir.

Barabas. Pray when, sir, shall I see you at my house?

Pilia-Borza. Soon enough to your cost, sir. Fare you well.

Exit.

Barabas. Nay, to thine own cost, villain, if thou comest.   60
    Was ever Jew tormented as I am?
    To have a shag-rag knave to come demand
    Three hundred crowns, and then five hundred crowns?
    Well, I must seek a means to rid 'em all,
    And presently, for in his villainy   65
    He will tell all he knows, and I shall die for 't.
    I have it.
    I will in some disguise go see the slave,
    And how the villain revels with my gold.   *Exit.*

[IV. iv]

Enter Courtesan [BELLAMIRA], ITHAMORE, [*and*] PILIA-BORZA.

Bellamira. I'll pledge thee, love, and therefore drink it off.

Ithamore. Say'st thou me so? Have at it; and do you hear?

[He whispers.]

Bellamira. Go to, it shall be so.

Ithamore. Of that condition I will drink it up. Here's to thee.

[He drinks.]

Bellamira. Nay, I'll have all or none.   5

Ithamore. There. If thou lov'st me, do not leave a drop.

Bellamira. Love thee? Fill me three glasses!

Ithamore. Three and fifty dozen I'll pledge thee.

Pilia-Borza. Knavely spoke, and like a knight at arms.

---

62. *shag-rag*] ragged, rascally.
    demand] not in Q; the phrase might also be 'convey', 'and fetch', etc.

IV.iv.1. *pledge*] offer a toast to.
    2.1. He whispers] Presumably Ithamore is making arrangements to sleep with Bellamira.
    4. *Of*] on.
    5.] i.e. 'I insist that you finish your glass.' She is getting him drunk. (The line is assigned in Q to *Pil.*, seemingly in error.)
    6.] Ithamore downs his drink and bids her do the same.
    9. *Knavely*] (playing on the familiar antithesis of 'knave' and 'knight').

Ithamore. Hey, *Rivo Castiliano!* A man's a man.   10
Bellamira. Now to the Jew.
Ithamore. Ha, to the Jew! And send me money, you were best.
Pilia-Borza. What wouldst thou do if he should send thee
     none?
Ithamore. Do nothing; but I know what I know. He's a   15
     murderer.
Bellamira. I had not thought he had been so brave a man.
Ithamore. You knew Mathias and the governor's son. He and
     I killed 'em both, and yet never touched 'em.
Pilia-Borza. Oh, bravely done!   20
Ithamore. I carried the broth that poisoned the nuns, and he
     and I—snickle, hand to! fast!—strangled a friar.
Bellamira. You two alone?
Ithamore. We two; and 'twas never known, nor never shall be
     for me.   25
Pilia-Borza. [*Aside to Bellamira*]
     This shall with me unto the governor.
Bellamira. [*To Pilia-Borza*]
     And fit it should; but first let's ha' more gold.—
     Come, gentle Ithamore, lie in my lap.
Ithamore. Love me little, love me long. Let music rumble,
     Whilst I in thy incony lap do tumble.   30

          Enter BARABAS *with a lute, disguised.*

Bellamira. A French musician! Come, let's hear your skill.
Barabas. Must tuna my lute for sound, twang, twang, first.
                                                    [*He tunes.*]

---

   10. Rivo Castiliano!] i.e. 'Let the drink flow'. The pseudo-Spanish is
uncertain in exact meaning, but the whole line is drunken braggadocio.
   11. *to*] (1) let's drink to; (2) let's write another letter to.
   12.] Ithamore threatens the absent Barabas and composes in his mind a
dunning letter.
   you were best] if you know what's good for you. Compare IV.ii.114.
   22. *snickle, hand to! fast!*] put the noose over his head! hold fast! snug!
   25. *for me*] as far as I'm concerned.
   29. *Love . . . long*] (proverbial, perhaps a song).
   30. *incony*] fine, delicate; with an obscene pun on 'in-cunny', in a woman's
lap.
   32. *Must tuna*] I must tune. Barabas is here represented as speaking with
a heavy French accent.

Ithamore. Wilt drink, Frenchman? Here's to thee with a—Pox
    on this drunken hiccup!
Barabas. Gramercy, monsieur.   35
Bellamira. Prithee, Pilia-Borza, bid the fiddler give me the
    posy in his hat there.
Pilia-Borza. Sirrah, you must give my mistress your posy.
Barabas. *A vôtre commandement,* madame. [*He gives a nosegay.*]
Bellamira. How sweet, my Ithamore, the flowers smell.   40
Ithamore. Like thy breath, sweetheart; no violet like 'em.
Pilia-Borza. Foh, methinks they stink like a hollyhock.
Barabas. [*Aside*] *So, now I am revenged upon 'em all.*
    The scent thereof was death; I poisoned it.
Ithamore. Play, fiddler, or I'll cut your cat's guts into chitter-   45
    lings.
Barabas. Pardonnez-moi, be no in tune yet. [*He tunes.*] So,
    now, now all be in.
Ithamore. Give him a crown, and fill me out more wine.
Pilia-Borza. [*Giving money*] There's two crowns for thee.   50
    Play.
Barabas. (*Aside*) *How liberally the villain gives me mine*
    own gold!
Pilia-Borza. Methinks he fingers very well.
Barabas. (*Aside*) *So did you when you stole my gold.*   55
Pilia-Borza. How swift he runs!
Barabas. (*Aside*) *You run swifter when you threw my gold out of*
    my window.
Bellamira. Musician, hast been in Malta long?
Barabas. Two, three, four month, madame.   60
Ithamore. Dost not know a Jew, one Barabas?

---

35. *Gramercy*] many thanks (French *Grand merci*).
37. *posy*] nosegay, small bouquet of flowers.
39.] 'At your command, madam.'
45. *cat's guts*] the lute strings.
45–6. *chitterlings*] the smaller intestines of beasts, e.g. pigs, used as food.
48. *in*] in tune.
49. *fill . . . wine*] pour more wine at my request.
53. *fingers very well*] skilfully fingers his lute. (But the next line suggests
another meaning: 'handles money with a thief's nimble fingers'.)
56. *runs*] plays a run or rapid sequence of notes (again with wordplay in
the next line, suggesting running away with stolen goods).

Barabas. Very mush, monsieur; you no be his man?

Pilia-Borza. His man?

Ithamore. I scorn the peasant, tell him so.

Barabas. [*Aside*] *He knows it already.*   65

Ithamore. 'Tis a strange thing of that Jew: he lives upon pickled grasshoppers and sauced mushrooms.

Barabas. (*Aside*) *What a slave's this! The governor feeds not
as I do.*

Ithamore. He never put on clean shirt since he was   70
circumcised.

Barabas. (*Aside*) *Oh, rascal! I change myself twice a day.*

Ithamore. The hat he wears Judas left under the elder when he
hanged himself.

Barabas. (*Aside*) *'Twas sent me for a present from the Great*   75
Cham.

Pilia-Borza. A musty slave he is.—Whither now, fiddler?

Barabas. *Pardonnez-moi*, monsieur, me be no well.   *Exit.*

Pilia-Borza. Farewell, fiddler.—One letter more to the Jew.

Bellamira. Prithee, sweet love, one more, and write it sharp.   80

Ithamore. No, I'll send by word of mouth now. Bid him
deliver thee a thousand crowns, by the same token that
the nuns loved rice, that Friar Bernardine slept in his own
clothes—any of 'em will do it.

Pilia-Borza. Let me alone to urge it, now I know the meaning.   85

Ithamore. The meaning has a meaning. Come, let's in.

To undo a Jew is charity and not sin.   *Exeunt.*

63.] Pilia-Borza scorns the idea of servitude, as does Ithamore in the next
line.

66–7. *pickled . . . mushrooms*] i.e. cheap and unappetizing food.

73–4.] According to a medieval tradition, Judas hanged himself on an
elder tree.

76. *Cham*] Khan.

77. *musty*] ill-humoured, peevish, dull, mouldy. Q's *masty*, 'burly,
fattened', is possible; the association of mast or acorns with swine would be
especially offensive to an orthodox Jew.

86. *The meaning . . . meaning*] Ithamore hints at profundity, of knowing
more than meets the eye.

Act V

[V. i]

Enter FERNEZE, Knights, MARTIN DEL BOSCO [, *and* Officers].

Ferneze. Now, gentlemen, betake you to your arms
    And see that Malta be well fortified.
    And it behoves you to be resolute;
    For Calymath, having hovered here so long,
    Will win the town or die before the walls.   5
First Knight. And die he shall, for we will never yield.

    Enter Courtesan [BELLAMIRA, *and*] PILIA-BORZA.

Bellamira. Oh, bring us to the governor.
Ferneze. Away with her. She is a courtesan.
Bellamira. Whate'er I am, yet, governor, hear me speak.
    I bring thee news by whom thy son was slain: 10
    Mathias did it not, it was the Jew.
Pilia-Borza. Who, besides the slaughter of these gentlemen,
    poisoned his own daughter and the nuns, strangled a
    friar, and I know not what mischief beside.
Ferneze. Had we but proof of this!   15
Bellamira.
    Strong proof, my lord. His man's now at my lodging
    That was his agent; he'll confess it all.
Ferneze. Go fetch him straight. [*Exeunt* Officers.] I always
    feared that Jew.

    Enter [Officers *with* BARABAS *the*] *Jew,* [*and*] ITHAMORE.

Barabas. I'll go alone. Dogs, do not hale me thus.
Ithamore. Nor me neither. I cannot outrun you, constable.   20
    Oh, my belly!

    V.i.4. *hovered*] waited near a particular point. (A naval term.)
    18. *feared*] mistrusted.
    21. *Oh, my belly!*] Ithamore is experiencing the violent effects of the
poison.

101

Barabas. [*Aside*] One dram of powder more had made all sure.
     What a damned slave was I!
Ferneze. Make fires, heat irons, let the rack be fetched.
First Knight. Nay, stay, my lord. 'T may be he will confess.   25
Barabas.
     Confess! What mean you, lords, who should confess?
Ferneze. Thou and thy Turk. 'Twas you that slew my son.
Ithamore. Guilty, my lord, I confess. Your son and Mathias
     were both contracted unto Abigail; he forged a counter-
     feit challenge.   30
Barabas. Who carried that challenge?
Ithamore. I carried it, I confess, but who writ it? Marry, even
     he that strangled Bernardine, poisoned the nuns and his
     own daughter.
Ferneze. Away with him! His sight is death to me.   35
Barabas. For what? You men of Malta, hear me speak.
     She is a courtesan, and he a thief,
     And he my bondman. Let me have law;
     For none of this can prejudice my life.
Ferneze. Once more, away with him!—You shall have law.   40
Barabas. Devils, do your worst; I'll live in spite of you.
     As these have spoke, so be it to their souls.
     [*Aside*] I hope the poisoned flowers will work anon.
     Exeunt [Officers *with* BARABAS, ITHAMORE, BELLAMIRA,
                                        and PILIA-BORZA].

                    Enter KATHERINE.

Katherine. Was my Mathias murdered by the Jew?
     Ferneze, 'twas thy son that murdered him.   45
Ferneze. Be patient, gentle madam; it was he.
     He forged the daring challenge made them fight.

---

35. *him*] Barabas.
38. *bondman*] slave.
law] a fair trial.
39.] i.e. 'I legally do not need to answer the accusations of my own slave
and his cohorts.' A slave-owner enjoyed this privilege in medieval law.
40. *law*] the full penalty of the law (playing sardonically on Barabas's
request for a fair trial, *law*, in l. 38).
42.] 'May their souls feel the torment that their words deserve.'
47. *daring*] issuing a dare.
made] that made.

Katherine. Where is the Jew? Where is that murderer?
Ferneze. In prison, till the law has passed on him.

Enter [First] Officer.

First Officer. My lord, the courtesan and her man are dead;   50
    So is the Turk, and Barabas the Jew.
Ferneze. Dead?
First Officer. Dead, my lord, and here they bring his body.

[*Enter* Officers, *carrying* BARABAS *as dead.*]

Bosco. This sudden death of his is very strange.
Ferneze. Wonder not at it, sir; the heavens are just.   55
    Their deaths were like their lives. Then think not of 'em.
    Since they are dead, let them be buried.
    For the Jew's body, throw that o'er the walls
    To be a prey for vultures and wild beasts.
                      [BARABAS *is thrown down.*]
    So; now away, and fortify the town.   60
                     Exeunt [*all but* BARABAS].
Barabas. [*Rising*] What, all alone? Well fare, sleepy drink!
    I'll be revengèd on this accursèd town,
    For by my means Calymath shall enter in.
    I'll help to slay their children and their wives,
    To fire the churches, pull their houses down;   65
    Take my goods too, and seize upon my lands.
    I hope to see the governor a slave,
    And, rowing in a galley, whipped to death.

Enter CALYMATH, Bashaws, [*and*] Turks.

Calymath. Whom have we there, a spy?
Barabas. Yes, my good lord, one that can spy a place   70
    Where you may enter and surprise the town.

---

    49. *passed*] passed sentence.
    58. *For*] as for.
    59.1.] Probably Barabas is thrown to one side, to signify that he has been pitched over the walls.
    61. *Well fare*] i.e. 'Here's to you!' Barabas offers thanks for the sleeping draught that has saved his life.
    66. *Take*] take back.
    71. *surprise*] take by surprise.

My name is Barabas; I am a Jew.

Calymath. Art thou that Jew whose goods we heard were sold
 For tribute-money?

Barabas.   The very same, my lord.
 And since that time they have hired a slave, my man, 75
 To accuse me of a thousand villainies.
 I was imprisoned, but escaped their hands.

Calymath. Didst break prison?

Barabas. No, no.
 I drank of poppy and cold mandrake juice, 80
 And, being asleep, belike they thought me dead,
 And threw me o'er the walls. So, or how else,
 The Jew is here, and rests at your command.

Calymath. 'Twas bravely done. But tell me, Barabas,
 Canst thou, as thou reportest, make Malta ours? 85

Barabas. Fear not, my lord; for here, against the sluice,
 The rock is hollow, and of purpose digged
 To make a passage for the running streams
 And common channels of the city.
 Now whilst you give assault unto the walls, 90
 I'll lead five hundred soldiers through the vault
 And rise with them i' the middle of the town,
 Open the gates for you to enter in,
 And by this means the city is your own.

Calymath. If this be true, I'll make thee governor. 95

Barabas. And if it be not true, then let me die.

Calymath. Thou'st doomed thyself. Assault it presently.

           Exeunt.

---

81. *belike*] perchance.
82. *So . . . else*] through those circumstances, or somehow.
83. *rests*] remains.
86. *against the sluice*] right next to the valve or gate in the sewer channel.
(Q's 'Truce' for 'sluice' is probably a compositor's error.)
87. *of purpose*] on purpose.
89. *channels*] sewers.
91. *vault*] covered sewer drain.
92. *rise*] come up out of the sewer.
97. *Thou'st doomed*] you have passed sentence on.

[v. ii]

> *Alarms. Enter* [CALYMATH,] Turks, [*and*] BARABAS, [*with*]
> FERNEZE *and* Knights *prisoners.*

Calymath. Now vail your pride, you captive Christians,
　　And kneel for mercy to your conquering foe.
　　Now where's the hope you had of haughty Spain?
　　Ferneze, speak: had it not been much better
　　To keep thy promise than be thus surprised?　　　　　5
Ferneze. What should I say? We are captives and must yield.
Calymath. Ay, villains, you must yield, and under Turkish
　　yokes
　　Shall groaning bear the burden of our ire;
　　And Barabas, as erst we promised thee,
　　For thy desert we make thee governor.　　　　　　10
　　Use them at thy discretion.
Barabas.　　　　　　　　　　Thanks, my lord.
Ferneze. O fatal day, to fall into the hands
　　Of such a traitor and unhallowed Jew!
　　What greater misery could heaven inflict?
Calymath. 'Tis our command; and, Barabas, we give,　　15
　　To guard thy person, these our Janizaries.
　　Entreat them well, as we have usèd thee.
　　And now, brave bashaws, come, we'll walk about
　　The ruined town and see the wrack we made.
　　Farewell, brave Jew, farewell, great Barabas.　　　20
Barabas. May all good fortune follow Calymath!
　　　　　　　　　　Exeunt [CALYMATH *and* Bashaws].
　　And now, as entrance to our safety,
　　To prison with the governor and these
　　Captains, his consorts and confederates.

V.ii.1. *vail*] humble, as in lowering sail as a token of deference.
3. *the hope . . . Spain*] See II.ii.40–1.
5. *surprised*] taken by surprise, as at V.i.71.
9. *erst*] just now.
11. *them*] the captive Maltese warriors.
16. *Janizaries*] an elite corps of Turkish infantry.
17. *Entreat*] treat.
19. *wrack*] destruction.
22. *entrance . . . safety*] the first step in making ourselves secure.
24. *consorts*] companions.

Ferneze. O villain, heaven will be revenged on thee!   25
Barabas. Away, no more! Let him not trouble me.

          Exeunt [Turks *with* FERNEZE *and* Knights].

    Thus hast thou gotten, by thy policy,
    No simple place, no small authority:
    I now am governor of Malta. True,
    But Malta hates me, and, in hating me,   30
    My life's in danger; and what boots it thee,
    Poor Barabas, to be the governor,
    Whenas thy life shall be at their command?
    No, Barabas, this must be looked into;
    And since by wrong thou got'st authority,   35
    Maintain it bravely by firm policy,
    At least unprofitably lose it not.
    For he that liveth in authority,
    And neither gets him friends nor fills his bags,
    Lives like the ass that Aesop speaketh of,   40
    That labours with a load of bread and wine
    And leaves it off to snap on thistle tops.
    But Barabas will be more circumspect.
    Begin betimes; Occasion's bald behind;
    Slip not thine opportunity, for fear too late   45
    Thou seek'st for much but canst not compass it.—
    Within here!

          Enter FERNEZE *with a* Guard.

Ferneze. My lord?

---

    27. *thou*] Barabas addresses himself.
    28. *simple*] humble, unpretentious.
    31. *boots*] avails.
    33. *Whenas*] seeing that.
    36–7.] 'hold on to that authority successfully by astute manipulation, or at least don't give it up without gaining some real advantage and profit'.
    40–2.] Asses proverbially labour for others' advantage.
    44.] 'Begin quickly, remembering that Occasion traditionally has a long forelock that one must seize at once because she is bald at the back of her head.' One gets only one chance.
    45. *Slip*] lose, neglect.
    46. *compass*] devise, contrive.
    47.1. with a *Guard*] under guard.

Barabas. [*Aside*] *Ay, 'lord'. Thus slaves will learn.*—
    Now, governor, stand by there.—Wait within!   50
                              [*Exit* Guard.]
      This is the reason that I sent for thee:
      Thou seest thy life, and Malta's happiness,
      Are at my arbitrament, and Barabas
      At his discretion may dispose of both.
      Now tell me, governor, and plainly too,   55
      What think'st thou shall become of it and thee?
Ferneze. This, Barabas: since things are in thy power,
      I see no reason but of Malta's wrack,
      Nor hope of thee but extreme cruelty;
      Nor fear I death, nor will I flatter thee.   60
Barabas. Governor, good words! Be not so furious;
      'Tis not thy life which can avail me aught.
      Yet you do live, and live for me you shall,
      And as for Malta's ruin, think you not
      'Twere slender policy for Barabas   65
      To dispossess himself of such a place?
      For sith, as once you said, within this isle,
      In Malta here, that I have got my goods,
      And in this city still have had success,
      And now at length am grown your governor,   70
      Yourselves shall see it shall not be forgot;
      For as a friend not known but in distress
      I'll rear up Malta, now remediless.
Ferneze. Will Barabas recover Malta's loss?
      Will Barabas be good to Christians?   75

50.] Barabas orders Ferneze to stand where he is while the guard retires.
53. *at my arbitrament*] subject to my decisions.
58.] 'I see nothing to expect but Malta's destruction.'
59. *extreme*] (accented on the first syllable)
61. *good words*] speak moderately (as at IV.iii.25).
63. *Yet*] still.
    for me] as far as I'm concerned (as at IV.iv.25).
65. *slender policy*] stupid stratagem.
67–8. *sith . . . that*] since.
68. *got my goods*] acquired my wealth.
72.] i.e. 'For, as a friend in need'.
73. *rear up*] raise up, relieve from distress.
    remediless] without hope of remedy, in a desperate position.

Barabas. What wilt thou give me, governor, to procure
      A dissolution of the slavish bands
      Wherein the Turk hath yoked your land and you?
      What will you give me if I render you
      The life of Calymath, surprise his men,   80
      And in an outhouse of the city shut
      His soldiers till I have consumed 'em all with fire?
      What will you give him that procureth this?
Ferneze. Do but bring this to pass which thou pretendest,
      Deal truly with us as thou intimatest,   85
      And I will send amongst the citizens
      And by my letters privately procure
      Great sums of money for thy recompense.
      Nay, more: do this, and live thou governor still.
Barabas. Nay, do thou this, Ferneze, and be free.   90
      Governor, I enlarge thee. Live with me,
      Go walk about the city, see thy friends.
      Tush, send not letters to 'em, go thyself,
      And let me see what money thou canst make.
      Here is my hand that I'll set Malta free.   95
      And thus we cast it: to a solemn feast
      I will invite young Selim Calymath,
      Where be thou present only to perform
      One stratagem that I'll impart to thee,
      Wherein no danger shall betide thy life,   100
      And I will warrant Malta free for ever.
Ferneze. Here is my hand. Believe me, Barabas,
      I will be there and do as thou desirest.
      When is the time?
Barabas.   Governor, presently.
      For Calymath, when he hath viewed the town,   105

---

77. *slavish*] enslaving.
79. *render*] hand over, deliver.
81. *outhouse*] i.e. building outside the city walls.
83. *procureth*] achieves.
84. *pretendest*] claim to be able to do; propose.
91. *enlarge*] set free.
94. *make*] gather, raise.
96. *cast*] devise, design, calculate.
solemn] ceremonial.
100. *betide*] happen to.

Will take his leave and sail toward Ottoman.
Ferneze. Then will I, Barabas, about this coin,
    And bring it with me to thee in the evening.
Barabas. Do so, but fail not. Now farewell, Ferneze.
                                                    [*Exit* FERNEZE.]
    And thus far roundly goes the business.   110
    Thus, loving neither, will I live with both,
    Making a profit of my policy;
    And he from whom my most advantage comes
    Shall be my friend.
    This is the life we Jews are used to lead,   115
    And reason, too, for Christians do the like.
    Well, now about effecting this device:
    First, to surprise great Selim's soldiers,
    And then to make provision for the feast,
    That at one instant all things may be done.   120
    My policy detests prevention.
    To what event my secret purpose drives,
    I know; and they shall witness with their lives.   *Exit.*

[v. iii]

                    Enter CALYMATH [*and*] Bashaws.

Calymath. Thus have we viewed the city, seen the sack,
    And caused the ruins to be new repaired,
    Which with our bombards' shot and basilisks'
    We rent in sunder at our entry,
    Two lofty turrets that command the town.   5
    And now I see the situation,
    And how secure this conquered island stands—
    Environed with the Mediterranean sea,

---

106. *Ottoman*] Turkey, or, the Turkish emperor.
107. *about this coin*] get to work raising the money.
110. *roundly*] briskly.
121.] 'Being anticipated by the enemy is anathema to my cunning design.'
123. *I know*] I alone know.
lives] i.e. deaths.

V.iii.1. *seen the sack*] witnessed the plundering of the city.
3. *bombards'* . . . *basilisks'*] shot of our various types of cannon.

Strong countermured with other petty isles,
And toward Calabria backed by Sicily,   10
Where Syracusian Dionysius reigned—
I wonder how it could be conquered thus.

Enter a Messenger.

Messenger. From Barabas, Malta's governor, I bring
    A message unto mighty Calymath.
    Hearing his sovereign was bound for sea,   15
    To sail to Turkey, to great Ottoman,
    He humbly would entreat your majesty
    To come and see his homely citadel
    And banquet with him ere thou leav'st the isle.
Calymath. To banquet with him in his citadel?   20
    I fear me, messenger, to feast my train
    Within a town of war so lately pillaged
    Will be too costly and too troublesome.
    Yet would I gladly visit Barabas,
    For well has Barabas deserved of us.   25
Messenger. Selim, for that, thus saith the governor:
    That he hath in store a pearl so big,
    So precious, and withal so orient,
    As, be it valued but indifferently,
    The price thereof will serve to entertain   30
    Selim and all his soldiers for a month.
    Therefore he humbly would entreat your highness
    Not to depart till he has feasted you.
Calymath. I cannot feast my men in Malta walls,
    Except he place his tables in the streets.   35

---

9. *countermured*] fortified with a double wall. (Q reads 'contermin'd';
compare I.ii.384.)
11. *Dionysius*] probably Dionysius the Elder, a notorious Sicilian tyrant,
405–367 B.C., often mentioned in sixteenth-century discussions of tyranny.
12. *thus*] i.e. so easily by us.
21. *train*] followers, soldiers.
26. *for that*] as for that.
29. *be . . . indifferently*] even if it did not realise its true value.
35. *Except*] unless.

Messenger. Know, Selim, that there is a monastery
    Which standeth as an outhouse to the town;
    There will he banquet them, but thee at home,
    With all thy bashaws and brave followers.
Calymath. Well, tell the governor we grant his suit.   40
    We'll in this summer evening feast with him.
Messenger. I shall, my lord.   *Exit.*
Calymath. And now, bold bashaws, let us to our tents,
    And meditate how we may grace us best
    To solemnize our governor's great feast.   *Exeunt.* 45

[v. iv]

      Enter FERNEZE, Knights, [*and* MARTIN] DEL BOSCO.

Ferneze. In this, my countrymen, be ruled by me:
    Have special care that no man sally forth
    Till you shall hear a culverin discharged
    By him that bears the linstock, kindled thus;
    Then issue out and come to rescue me,   5
    For happily I shall be in distress,
    Or you releasèd of this servitude.
First Knight. Rather than thus to live as Turkish thralls,
    What will we not adventure?
Ferneze. On then, be gone.
Knights.   Farewell, grave governor.   10
                        [*Exeunt.*]

---

44. *grace us*] adorn ourselves, ready ourselves.

V.iv.3. *culverin*] long-muzzled cannon.
  4. *linstock*] staff with a forked head to hold a lighted match, used to ignite cannon.
  6. *happily*] perchance.
  7.] 'or if I am in no trouble, you will be released of Turkish domination and your duty will have been duly discharged'.
  8. *thralls*] slaves, captives.
  9. *adventure*] risk, attempt.
  10. *grave*] honoured, noble.

[v. v]

> *Enter* [BARABAS] *with a hammer above, very busy*[,
> *and* Carpenters].

Barabas. How stand the cords? How hang these hinges, fast?
   Are all the cranes and pulleys sure?
Carpenter.   All fast.
Barabas. Leave nothing loose, all levelled to my mind.
   Why, now I see that you have art indeed.
   There, carpenters, divide that gold amongst you.   5
                              [*He gives money.*]
   Go swill in bowls of sack and muscadine;
   Down to the cellar, taste of all my wines.
Carpenters. We shall, my lord, and thank you.
                              Exeunt [Carpenters].
Barabas. And if you like them, drink your fill—and die;
   For, so I live, perish may all the world.   10
   Now, Selim Calymath, return me word
   That thou wilt come, and I am satisfied.

> *Enter* Messenger.

   Now sirrah, what, will he come?
Messenger. He will; and has commanded all his men
   To come ashore and march through Malta streets,   15
   That thou mayst feast them in thy citadel.   [*Exit.*]
Barabas. Then now are all things as my wish would have 'em.
   There wanteth nothing but the governor's pelf—

> *Enter* FERNEZE.

   And see, he brings it.—Now, governor, the sum?
Ferneze. With free consent, a hundred thousand pounds.   20

V.v.o.1. *above*] i.e. in the gallery of his house (fitted for this scene with a
trap door).
   3. *all . . . mind*] all carefully constructed according to my specifications.
   6. *sack and muscadine*] white Spanish wine and muscatel.
   9. *die*] i.e. (1) die from wine poisoned to get rid of witnesses, or (2) die
when you will, for all I care.
   10. *so*] provided that.
   18. *pelf*] money.

Barabas. Pounds, say'st thou, governor? Well, since it is no
  more,
  I'll satisfy myself with that; nay, keep it still,
  For if I keep not promise, trust not me.
  And, governor, now partake my policy.
  First, for his army: they are sent before,   25
  Entered the monastery, and underneath
  In several places are field-pieces pitched,
  Bombards, whole barrels full of gunpowder,
  That on the sudden shall dissever it
  And batter all the stones about their ears,   30
  Whence none can possibly escape alive.
  Now, as for Calymath and his consorts,
  Here have I made a dainty gallery,
  The floor whereof, this cable being cut,
  Doth fall asunder, so that it doth sink   35
  Into a deep pit past recovery.
       [He throws down a knife to Ferneze.]
  Here, hold that knife, and when thou seest he comes,
  And with his bashaws shall be blithely set,
  A warning-piece shall be shot off from the tower
  To give thee knowledge when to cut the cord   40
  And fire the house. Say, will not this be brave?
Ferneze. Oh, excellent! Here, hold thee, Barabas.
           [He offers the money.]
  I trust thy word; take what I promised thee.
Barabas. No, governor, I'll satisfy thee first.
  Thou shalt not live in doubt of anything.   45
  Stand close, for here they come. *[FERNEZE retires.]*
         Why, is not this
  A kingly kind of trade, to purchase towns
  By treachery and sell 'em by deceit?

---

24. *partake my policy*] be acquainted with my scheme.
25. *for*] as for.
28. *Bombards*] cannon, as at V.iii.3.
29. *dissever*] shatter.
33. *dainty*] intricately wrought.
38. *blithely set*] cheerfully seated at table.
39. *A warning-piece*] a gun fired as a signal or alarm.
41. *fire the house*] i.e. set off explosives underneath the monastery.

Now tell me, worldlings, underneath the sun
If greater falsehood ever has been done.   50

Enter CALYMATH *and* Bashaws.

Calymath. Come, my companion bashaws, see, I pray,
          How busy Barabas is there above
          To entertain us in his gallery.
          Let us salute him.—Save thee, Barabas!
Barabas. Welcome, great Calymath.   55
Ferneze. [*Aside*] *How the slave jeers at him!*
Barabas. Will 't please thee, mighty Selim Calymath,
          To ascend our homely stairs?
Calymath.   Ay, Barabas.
          Come, bashaws, attend.
Ferneze. [*Coming forward*]   Stay, Calymath,
          For I will show thee greater courtesy   60
          Than Barabas would have afforded thee.
Knight. [*Within*] Sound a charge there!

        A charge [*sounded*], *the cable cut, a cauldron discovered*
                [*into which* BARABAS *has fallen*].
          [*Enter* MARTIN DEL BOSCO *and* Knights.]

Calymath. How now, what means this?
Barabas. Help, help me, Christians, help!
Ferneze. See, Calymath, this was devised for thee.   65
Calymath. Treason, treason! Bashaws, fly!
Ferneze. No, Selim, do not fly;
          See his end first, and fly then if thou canst.
Barabas. Oh, help me, Selim, help me, Christians!
          Governor, why stand you all so pitiless?   70
Ferneze. Should I in pity of thy plaints or thee,
          Accursèd Barabas, base Jew, relent?

---

49. *worldlings*] Barabas sardonically addresses the audience as persons
devoted to self-promotion, asking for their admiration.

62. *charge*] trumpet call presumably sounded as a signal that the cannon is
to fire and Ferneze's men are to come to his rescue, as he ordered at V.iv.1–
7.

62.1. discovered] revealed in the theatre by the opening of a curtain or
some such device.

    No, thus I'll see thy treachery repaid,
    But wish thou hadst behaved thee otherwise.
Barabas. You will not help me, then?
Ferneze.   No, villain, no.   75
Barabas. And, villains, know you cannot help me now.
    Then, Barabas, breathe forth thy latest fate,
    And in the fury of thy torments strive
    To end thy life with resolution.
    Know, governor, 'twas I that slew thy son;   80
    I framed the challenge that did make them meet.
    Know, Calymath, I aimed thy overthrow,
    And, had I but escaped this stratagem,
    I would have brought confusion on you all,
    Damned Christian dogs and Turkish infidels!   85
    But now begins the extremity of heat
    To pinch me with intolerable pangs.
    Die, life: fly, soul; tongue, curse thy fill and die!
                            [*He dies.*]
Calymath. Tell me, you Christians, what doth this portend?
Ferneze. This train he laid to have entrapped thy life.   90
    Now, Selim, note the unhallowed deeds of Jews.
    Thus he determined to have handled thee;
    But I have rather chose to save thy life.
Calymath. Was this the banquet he prepared for us?
    Let's hence, lest further mischief be pretended.   95
Ferneze. Nay, Selim, stay, for since we have thee here,
    We will not let thee part so suddenly.
    Besides, if we should let thee go, all's one,
    For with thy galleys couldst thou not get hence
    Without fresh men to rig and furnish them.   100
Calymath. Tush, governor, take thou no care for that.
    My men are all aboard,
    And do attend my coming there by this.

---

77. *thy latest fate*] the last moments of life that fate allows.
81. *framed*] composed.
82. *aimed*] planned, intended.
89. *portend*] mean.
90. *train*] plot.
95. *pretended*] intended, offered.
98. *all's one*] it would make no difference.

Ferneze. Why, heard'st thou not the trumpet sound a charge?
Calymath. Yes. What of that?
Ferneze.   Why, then the house was fired,   105
  Blown up, and all thy soldiers massacred.
Calymath. Oh, monstrous treason!
Ferneze.   A Jew's courtesy;
  For he that did by treason work our fall
  By treason hath delivered thee to us.
  Know, therefore, till thy father hath made good   110
  The ruins done to Malta and to us,
  Thou canst not part; for Malta shall be freed
  Or Selim ne'er return to Ottoman.
Calymath. Nay, rather, Christians, let me go to Turkey,
  In person there to meditate your peace.   115
  To keep me here will naught advantage you.
Ferneze. Content thee, Calymath, here thou must stay
  And live in Malta prisoner; for come all the world
  To rescue thee, so will we guard us now
  As sooner shall they drink the ocean dry   120
  Than conquer Malta or endanger us.
  So, march away, and let due praise be given
  Neither to fate nor fortune, but to heaven.   [*Exeunt.*]

FINIS.

---

115. *meditate*] negotiate. (Perhaps it should read *mediate*.)